TE

My Year 2005:

Terrifying Times

READINGS
EVENTS
MEMORIES

by
Douglas Messerli

GREEN INTEGER
KØBENHAVN & LOS ANGELES
2006

GREEN INTEGER BOOKS
Edited by Per Bregne
København / Los Angeles

Distributed in the United States by Consortium Book
Sales and Distribution, 1045 Westgate Drive, Suite 90
Saint Paul, Minnesota 55114-1065
Distributed in England and throughout Europe by
Turnaround Publisher Services
Unit 3, Olympia Trading Estate
Coburg Road, Wood Green, London N22 6TZ
44 (0)20 88293009

(323) 857-1115 / http://www.greeninteger.com

First Green Integer Edition 2006
Copyright ©2006 by Douglas Messerli
Essays in this volume have previously appeared in
The American Book Review, ArtXpress,
The Golden Handcuffs Review, The Green Integer Review,
Jacket, and *The New Review of Literature*
Back cover copy ©2006 by Green Integer

Design: Per Bregne
Typography: Yuko Sawamoto
Cover photograph: [clockwise from left to right]
Stacey Levine (Daniel Morris/Fat Yehti), Jonas Lie,
Alfred Hitchcock and Robert Creeley

LIBRARY OF CONGRESS CATALOGING IN PUBLICATION DATA
Messerli, Douglas [1947]
My Year 2005: Terrifying Times
ISBN: 1-933382-65-1
Green Integer 260
I. Title II. Series.

Green Integer books are published for Douglas Messerli
Printed in the United States on acid-free paper

Table Of Contents

An Introduction of Sorts

This is a strange project: an account of my own life, going back in time, while simultaneously stepping forward, at a rate of two volumes each year until 2010, when I will continue into the future. Some may see this as a self-promoting exercise, but I feel it is quite the opposite, so perhaps to bear out this assertion I need to explain.

For several years now, some of my friends, Mac Wellman and Dennis Phillips in particular, have been pushing me to write my memoirs. Mac has long argued that our generation has failed to offer younger generations a testimony to what we have done and how we have done it. And Dennis tells me that what I write might be of interest to readers.

There is no doubt that as a writer and publisher with a background in music and dance, and whose companion is a curator of contemporary art at a major museum, I have been lucky enough to know some of the most interesting creative beings of the century. I have had the opportunity to meet Djuna Barnes, Kenneth Burke, and Eudora Welty; to take a course in creative writing with Isaac B. Singer;

and to print the work of many authors (Kay Boyle, Barbara Guest, and Marianne Hauser among others), whose careers had been established long before I was even contemplating art. But writing a memoir seemed—and does still today—to be nearly impossible.

Perhaps in order to write about oneself one has to have a sense of coherence in one's life. My senior editor, Diana Daves, for example, remembers nearly all of her high school and college classmates, and has kept in close touch with many of them over the years. Although my parents appeared to me as quite steady folk, I counted one day that I had lived as a young child in approximately nine different homes in four different towns before I even left high school during my senior year to live in Norway. While I was away, my parents moved twice more, and when I returned they moved to four or five other homes before settling into the house in which my mother still lives. I grew up in Iowa, but graduated from a small city in Wisconsin, attended two universities there, ran away to live in New York City twice, and escaped to Washington, D.C. and Maryland, where I settled long enough to accomplish the rest of my education. But even there, while living rather tranquilly with my companion, I lived in four different apartments. With each of these changes, moreover, I shed many former memories and forgot the names of numerous friends. Later, as a university professor I lived simultaneously in two cities, Philadelphia and Washington, D.C., and spent many of my weekends in either Baltimore or New York before finally moving to Los Angeles, where I have stolidly remained now for nearly twenty years.

This disjunctive past also explains, I suspect, why I write and produce work under several different pseudonyms: Kier Peters, Claude Ricochet, Joshua Haigh, Katie Messborn, and Per Bregne among them. I have long argued that we are all several people, and that the insistence of our society that we harbor these differing aspects of self in one coherent being only limits our potentialities. It's apparent at least to me that it would be nearly impossible for someone like to me to write about a single "life." No, I could not write a memoir, I insisted.

Yet I was intrigued. How can one speak of one's achievements—and I did feel that I had achieved something—and link it all up? Certainly there were memories, but I wasn't interested in simply writing about myself. I have come to realize over the years—in part because of my wanderlust and my purposeful confusion of identity—that I am interested in collaborative experiences rather than singular ones. What does one discover about oneself within a larger series of cultural experiences—musical, literary, performative, visual, and physical events that occur within one's lifetime within an international context? That, of course, must also include the past, as one tries to imagine or newly realize the experiences of others in the equally complex time gone by.

Suddenly one day I realized that I had already been chronicling some of these experiences in the several reviews, essays, and casual writings I had been doing year by year. In 2000, accordingly, I began collecting such essays along with new writings to be possibly published in two books—*Being American/Being UnAmerican*. The more I wrote of things I read, heard, saw, and contemplated, the richer I realized my life had been and was increasingly becoming. Before I knew it, I had written about so many works of fiction, poetry, film, theater, art, dance, music, television and, yes, personal experiences that there would obviously be no way to collect these in two volumes. What was interesting about the project, as I saw it, was not just to offer up a selection of the best of these pieces, but to present the process of living a recorded life day by day, or at least year by year. So the series before you, *My Year* _____ was born.

I immediately want to apologize to the reader who is seeking a coherent linking. He or she will find little connection among the essays printed in these pages. This volume, for example, begins with my reading a Norwegian novel from 1893 and ends with a review of an American fiction published in 2005; its only connecting theme is suggested by the subtitle, "Terrifying Times." I would argue that the experience and assimilation of culture is not a linear process, and these writings—formulated as a pastiche of readings, events and memories written about, experienced or published during one particular year, along with pieces from the past and future years that intuitively seemed appropriate—make no attempt to represent unity. As I set my personal "cradle" in motion, moving forward and backward in time (I plan volumes going back to at least the year 2000), I warn readers desperate for coherence that they will be frustrated by a lack of plot or even summarization. Perhaps only upon my death and the obvious completion of this experiment will one be able to say—ah, there's the story! But I doubt there will ever be any obvious resolution. The self I present in these pages is, at times, a bit frightening, revealing almost a maniacal drive to experience culture. But this same self, I would argue, can also be modest and self-deprecating. If at times I seem impatient and judgmental, I am, as I see it, joyfully engaged in the world around me. I seek no agreement with what I put forth and often have skewered my perceptions of things in order to explore issues that most interest me. I do also want to assure the reader, however, that as strange as some of the events described in these works may seem, I have attempted to be as honest as memory allows me to be. Everything I relate in these pages represents the truth as I have perceived it.

There are numerous such issues which I intend to explore, and already I can perceive the common denominator of many of these writings, that in its sheer energy, if nothing else, American culture — as well as that of the other cultures in the world — is filled with immense belief and serious doubt, with hypocrisy and inconsistencies that allow the ugly and the beautiful, evil and good to coexist — the important thing being to recognize them each for what they are! I find no easy answers in these numerous writings, but the questions I ask I hope are of importance for our times, times which — with devastating storms, fire and drought throughout large parts of the nation, and involvement in a continuing war — were definitely terrifying.

Such a massive undertaking inevitably includes the collaboration of numerous individuals, including all the authors, actors, dancers, visual artists, scholars and others mentioned in these pages. I have already reported that these ongoing cultural memoirs had their impetus in conversations with Mac Wellman and Dennis Phillips. Will Alexander, Thérèse Bachand, Charles Bernstein, Diana Daves, Deborah Meadows, Martin Nakell, Paul Vangelisti and my companion, Howard Fox also encouraged me in this project and were patient enough to read some of these entries and listen to my personal recountings. The many editors of the journals and on-line publications in which these pieces first appeared often focused my attention on certain works and helped to hone my writing style. Ann Klefstad carefully edited the final drafts, and brought clarity and grammatical structure to the various pieces. Yuko Sawamoto brought these pages to life through her many talents in design and typography.

How to Destroy Your Children

JONAS LIE **NIOBE** (KØBENHAVN: GLYDENDAL, 1893).
TRANSLATED FROM THE NORWEGIAN BY H. L.
BRÆKSTAD (LONDON: W. HEINEMANN, 1897/NEW
YORK: GEORGE H. RICHMOND & SON, 1898)

Jonas Lie

Dr. Borvig and his family live a comfortable life in a small Norwegian town at the turn of the previous century. Like many in their financial position, they have the normal bourgeois aspirations for their children: that they get a good education (they have hired a tutor for the lower-level schooling of their children and have sent one of their sons to the university), that their children grow up to productive figures in the community of their choice. Borvig and his wife Bente, in short, appear like many modern couples, to have together and separately pampered and spoiled their offspring.

The son at the university, Endre, has changed his educational focus several times, abandoning, after three years, training for the Church to take up, instead, philology. As the novel opens Endre has written his mother—with whom he clearly has deeper ties than his father—that he has found his true avocation: singing. Borvig is outraged and refuses to send him more money, while his mother determines she shall help him by taking from her own savings.

The doctor feels fortunate that his other son— whom we soon discover is his own favorite—is successfully running a local mill. But Kjel also has hazy dreams of power, determining to ingratiate himself with local businessmen who might invest in his projects. We quickly see that his expenses from entertaining and gambling are even more costly than Endre's shifts in education. And later in the novel, when he convinces the father to invest in a timber deal, his shady dealings become apparent.

Minka, their teenage daughter, has her own problems: she is terribly bright but is also highly excitable. Living a life at once protected and, in educational terms, utterly progressive, she is confused by the issues now suddenly facing her regarding sexuality, politics (in the form of women's rights) and what used to be called the life of the imagination — a world of great music, art and literature. The tutor, Schulteiss — a slightly grotesque, hunchbacked figure — is secretly in love with his eldest pupil, and conspires with her mother to protect her innocence, which, at the same time, further pushes the young girl towards a world she intellectually conceives but knows little about.

The arrival of two outsiders, the fashionable and liberated writer Thelka Feiring (come to serve as governess of another local family) and Varberg, an engineer come to plan the new railroad, further stirs the waters at Elvsæt, the Borvig house. Thelka, admired even before her arrival by Minka, is a force of sunlight in the Borvig world; Kjel quickly charms her and they are married. Varberg, on the other hand, is a dark-eyed, menacing presence who affects everyone with a sense of paralyzing drowsiness. We soon discover, in fact, that Varberg believes in Mesmerism, spiritualism, and other "crackpot" theories that challenge the family's more conventional philosophies. His power over Minka is quickly noticed, and Schulteiss, in particular, ineffectively attempts to intervene.

The return home of Endre from the university, soon joined by friends, brings further tension into this innocent-seeming family, as one of his acquaintances, Finsland — himself a sort of intellectual fraud — is also attracted to Minka, and finds himself in intellectual combat with the taciturn Varberg. As Kjel and Thelka's marriage begins to disintegrate, and Borvig gradually must face the fact that his son is near financial disaster which, in turn, will involve him, through his loan, in the scandal, it becomes apparent that the doctor and his wife have indirectly created a three-headed monster in their children that can only terrorize them. A mysterious fire at the mill, protected by insurance, temporarily saves son and father from scandal. But the event breaks the older man, and he and his wife determine to protect their younger three children by sending them away to technical school for a more practical upbringing. A short time after, Borvig dies.

Endre, whose career as a singer has failed miserably, returns home for good, and Minka, having gone off in search of love, also returns, "uncontrollably nervous in her speech, sensitive in every fibre...," "Full of imbecile theories and notions...." Kjel's fraud, meanwhile, has been discovered by local authorities, and he faces "penal servitude." As the distressed family copes with Kjel's impending arrest and Endre's lack of a future, Minka reveals that she has agreed to marry Varberg, a decision over which, she claims, she has no control.

Recalling that her youngest son, Arnt, had left a tin box of dynamite cartridges in the lumber room, Mrs. Borvig, "with a wild cry of terror," strikes the box with an axe, the explosion leaving the house in ruins, "and among the logs and splinters...four crushed bodies—those of Mrs. Borvig and her three grown-up children."

Lie's grandly operatic novel is, at the same time, an acutely-tuned realist work that functions—given the backdrop of an everyday bourgeois family—as a believable psychological study in how children are destroyed by the very people who most love them. In the context of my discussions (in 2004) of Holden Caulfield, Lolita, and Malcolm, and of Hitchcock's film *Shadow of a Doubt* (in this same volume), we recognize that there are numerous forms of child abuse—among the worst is the blindly conventional, over-protective love of some families. It's not simply that these children were spoiled, that they were over-indulged, but that they were led into a real world with highly idealized concepts and aspirations which, when they did not accord with reality, forced them to react deceitfully and out of delusion.

Fin de siècle family life in Norway, we discover, was not so very different from American life in the 1950s—or even at the turn of the 21st century. Again and again we learn, reality cannot be perceived merely through ideals and education.

Los Angeles, September 15, 2005

Three Hitchcock Structures

THORNTON WILDER, SALLY BENSON, AND
ANNA REVILLE (WRITERS),
ALFRED HITCHCOCK (DIRECTOR)
SHADOW OF A DOUBT / 1943

The two Charlies, Joseph Cotton and Teresa Wright

A Horrifying Waltz

Over the past few years, I have come to realize that what interests me most about the films of Alfred Hitchcock is not simply that he is a brilliant director who produces some of the most dazzling images ever seen on film, but that he and his scriptwriters have a great interest in narrative structures—what we might describe in fiction or poetry as genre. This is nowhere more apparent than in his 1943 masterwork, *Shadow of a Doubt*.

Hitchcock couldn't have chosen more brilliant writers for this project. In addition to his wife, Anna Reville, who worked closely with him on many of his films, the film was scripted by one of the major American playwrights of the day, Thornton Wilder, writing just a few years after his classic *Our Town*, and by a figure who knew small-town America perhaps better than anyone, Sally Benson, whose *Kensington Stories* were the basis of *Meet Me in St. Louis* (a film which appeared the following year, and which she must have been working on during the shooting of or soon after *Shadow of a Doubt*); Benson later wrote film scripts such as *The Farmer Takes a Wife* and *Anna and the King of Siam*. The abilities of these three to present a near-perfect portrait of small-town USA matched Hitchcock's evident belief that evil, revenge, and murder coexisted always with innocence, love, and kindness.

The film demonstrates this theory in many ways, particularly in the comic episodes between Joseph Newton, father of the loving family at the center of the work, and his friend, Herbie Hawkins, who, at the very table where they will soon dine with a *real* murderer—Joseph's brother-in-law Charlie—plot the imaginary murders of each other.

But the important focus of this film is on Joseph's daughter, also named Charlie, a young woman, who, like most awakening teenagers, is absolutely bored by and frustrated with the family life into which she has been born. She is desperate for adventure and, in a highly intuitive act of frustration, visits the telegraph office to send her uncle Charlie, after whom she was named, a plea to come for a visit.

The audience already knows that this somewhat sinister figure is on his way at that very moment, and has just notified the family, through the same office, that he is soon to arrive. The coincidence is a haunting note in this otherwise normal-appearing world, for it becomes quickly clear that uncle and niece have more than their name in common, that indeed they are mysteriously intertwined with each other, the bond between them being much stronger than family blood and affection. We sense almost from the beginning that their relationship is a bit perverse, and Hitchcock and his writers take the story far deeper than any sexual attraction might allow, putting it on a level that is archetypal at the very least and almost mythic in its scope. As the young Charlie tells her uncle upon his arrival: "I know everything about you. You can't hide anything from me."

In short, we quickly sense in this film that these two, in their intricate interconnectedness, stand apart from the world they inhabit. They are a sort of Yin and Yang, female and male, young and old, innocent and evil, light and dark (although, in this, reversed from the Chinese model), truthteller and liar, believer and skeptic, one living in the present, the other in the past.

At the celebratory dinner for the uncle, young Charlie reveals that she cannot get a tune out of her head in connection with her uncle: *The Merry Window Waltz*. As in Orson Welles' *The Magnificent Ambersons*, shown in theaters the year before, the authors and director of *Shadow of a Doubt* take that theme as an emblem, almost, of their structure. The music and the accompanying waltz (montaged over the family center of the kitchen as young Charlie and her mother are about to serve dinner) becomes a sinister prefiguring of character action: the two Charlies, locked in another's arms, are doomed to dance until one or the other is dead!

A gift of a ring from her uncle — again signifying the symbolic "marriage" between them — sends the intuitive young girl into a spin as she discovers a name engraved within and quickly connects it with the page her uncle has torn from the newspaper. A quick trip to the library teaches this apt pupil information one hopes no child should ever have to learn: that the man to whom she is bonded, so to speak, is a murderer — *The Merry Widow* Murderer! (a name taken from the fact that he preys on elderly widowed women).

From that horrible moment of discovery to the end of the film, there is no turning back for this young, fresh, and believing girl, so touchingly portrayed by Teresa Wright: in her young dance of life and death she must endure and discover all the dark hate and evil of her uncle's being, just as he will recover (or at least claim the recovery of) some of the values of youth he has lost.

Until this moment, Uncle Charlie has been exhausted, unable to sleep; now suddenly his niece falls into a deep sleep from which she awakens only the next evening. What she must now face is the plotting of a real murder — her own — just as her father and friend mockingly playact murder and detection. Detectives indeed have already shown up at the Newton house, again masquerading as people who, like the uncle, are searching for the average American family. Once more, young Charlie sees through their deception, but as Uncle Charlie begins the attempts to murder her (a step of the back staircase of the house has been sawed through) and her uncle exposes her to his disgusting view of life, she is nearly desperate to keep the detectives near her.

The ring her uncle has given her is stolen; the symbolic "marriage," in short, is annulled. But the very fact that she now has no real evidence of his guilt, and her realization that accusations against her uncle would destroy her sentimentally inclined mother and forever change family life only force her to continue the appalling waltz. She too must now plot, recognize lies and greed in those around her. Nearly killed in her uncle's second attempt to murder her, she is forced to steal, recapturing the ring to assure the older Charlie's departure from their lives.

As Uncle Charlie is seen retiring to the train for a voyage away from the family, some may feel relief, but the astute viewers perceive that the dance is not quite over. Forced to remain on the train after it has pulled away from the station, the young Charlie must accept her partner in one more *galop* as, arms around her in dance-like position, her uncle attempts to push her off the train. Youth has no choice but to struggle against age and destroy it. Her uncle leaning out from the car is decapitated. If not in actuality, at least within the myth of the film, she has now also committed murder. She has been forced, to ensure her survival, to experience all the evil that he so horribly insisted was the condition of life.

In the awful last scene of this painful film, the young Charlie stands outside the church wherein her family and the community piously mourn the loss of her uncle, revealing her new social and metaphysical position. She has had her adventure, but she can never truly return to the innocence, love, and protection of her childhood home again.

Los Angeles, April 17, 2005

JOHN MICHAEL HAYES (WRITER),
ALFRED HITCHCOCK (DIRECTOR)
REAR WINDOW / 1954

View from the rear window

The Prisonhouse of Love

For most of years since I first saw Alfred Hitchcock's brilliant film, *Rear Window*, I had concluded — along with most of the commentators on that film — that the work was primarily about voyeurism, about a society of voyeurs, about a particular voyeur (L. B. Jefferies/James Stewart), and about the way voyeurism plays a role in the making and watching of films themselves. There is a kind of perversity about the work, and the fact that, as some commentators had noted, the "murderer" suddenly turns the tables, crashing out of the frame to attack Jefferies for the invasion of his privacy, allows one easily to characterize Hitchcock's film, like his later *Vertigo*, as a study in psychosis: that of character and audience alike.

Of course, everyone recognizes that there are important aspects to the film that take it in adventuresome and comic directions — such as the strangely distant relationship of Jefferies and Lisa Fremont (Grace Kelly) and Lisa and Stella's (Thelma Ritter) involvement with Jefferies' voyeurism. But the film long seemed to me a frightening statement on society's passive psycho-sexual propensities.

Increasingly over the past few years, however, I have felt that I was missing something in perceiving the movie only in this way. The writing (by John Michael Hayes), for example, is quite remarkably clever. And, despite the darkness of its overall concerns, there is more comedy in this work than in almost any Hitchcock film other than *The Trouble with Harry*.

Recently in revisiting the film, I observed that, despite Jefferies' vocation as a photographer—an accident in connection with his photography is why he stuck in the two-room apartment—he does not actually use his camera for the usual purposes. We do discover that he has taken photographs (he has pictures of the garden and comments on having taken "leg art" of the young woman across the way), but as audience we see him use the camera only as a kind of telescope—and, later, as the murderer comes calling, as a flash device to temporarily ward off attack.

It is obvious, indeed, that Jefferies is nearly impotent with his leg in a cast: he cannot, metaphorically speaking, use his "tool," the tool of his trade. Similarly, he cannot be sexually stimulated by one of the most beautiful and well-dressed women in the world—Lisa Fremont. As Stella observes, he can't even get a temperature—he is symbolically and, apparently, literally frigid, despite the heat wave disturbing all the other tenants and his visitors.

Moreover, he himself is *in camera*, trapped in a room not unlike a judge's chambers—where he *is* judged as a failure by both his nurse and would-be lover. Like the camera he uses he now exists in a kind of black box from which he cannot escape, and which, in turn, forces him to look outside of his own self and space.

It becomes quite apparent early in the film that L. B. Jefferies has no life other than that of nomadic observer of things. Like many American boy-men (a phenomenon on which I have commented elsewhere) he finds any suggestion that he "settle down" to be an unpleasant alternative he has no intention of accepting. His and Lisa's witty discussion of "here" and "there" is almost a treatise on the kind of meaningless life he has lived: she, the healthy sexual beauty, ready to offer up her body as a "free mount," is all "here," while Jefferies is only "there," anywhere but where love and social engagement exist.

Through the accident of his being laid up, Jefferies is forced to view what is around him; and that consists of various sexual and societal possibilities. Rather than focusing, as do most critics, on the window of the "murderer"—which takes the movie in the direction of the murder mystery genre which, argues one critic, Hitchcock settled on after presenting the possibility of others—it might be useful if we were to first consider the various tableaux presented to his major character.

There is the single, hard-of-hearing sculptor, a creative spirit who lives rather nicely by herself. But Hitchcock and, by extension, Jefferies presents her as a busybody. In this rear window tableaux, her satisfaction is the exception.

The woman living above her, Miss Torso, a shapely young girl who parties each evening, is seen by Jefferies as offering up, almost like a prostitute, her sexuality. Lisa perceives her, rather, as "juggling wolves," not at all interested in any of the men surrounding her each night. Ultimately, we discover that Lisa is right, for Miss Torso is delighted upon the return of her rather unattractive soldier boy.

Nearby lives "Miss Lonelyheart," a middle-aged woman who, unlike the sculptor, is not at all happy being alone; she sets the table for two and play-acts a visiting guest. At one point, when she actually brings home a stranger, his sexual advances force her to demand he leave, and she is left unhappily alone again. Both Stella and Jefferies are terrified that she may attempt suicide.

A composer, whom both Stella and Lisa admire, is described by Jefferies as a man living alone who "probably had a very unhappy marriage"; later he describes him as "getting it" (the topic is inspiration, but the subtext is sex) mostly from his landlady.

Also across the way a couple, to escape the heat, sleep on their balcony in full view of all, which clearly suggests that they do not have much of a love life; their major activity centers around hoisting their dog up and down into house and yard by means of a small basket, and when the dog is killed by the murderer, their grief is broadcast to all the neighbors.

A young married couple who briefly appear at another window spend days in bed apparently enjoying the sexual bliss of new matrimony. Jefferies similarly scoffs at their behavior.

Indeed, Jefferies is almost prudishly critical of all these individuals and their relationships with others.

But it is the "murderer" Lars Thorwald and his wife who most clearly represent what the observant prisoner perceives as the standard condition of a relationship—a nagging and bed-bound wife driving her seemingly patient salesman husband to distraction—and ultimately, of course, to murder.

In short, because of his enforced entombment in his "plaster cocoon," because of his temporary "imprisonment," (Stella claims in the very first scene to know that there is going to be "trouble" and that her patient will wind up in the New York state prison

Dannemora), Jefferies, locked in a prison of his own making, is forced to encounter the "here," the world of societal and sexual interrelationships. Despite the difficulty Lisa has in getting him to "mount," and to climb the symbolic mountain of her love, the "adventurer" must give up all action before he can discover how to behave. If he has previously lived only as a voyeur, as someone who clicks and snaps images of reality, he is now forced to truly observe and encouraged to involve himself in the world.

Of course, there is also a price to be paid for that involvement. Since he cannot function and cannot enter the world, Lisa enters it for him, endangering her own life. Lisa's illegal entry into the Thorwald's apartment and her discovery of the wife's wedding ring forces Jefferies to perceive his failures. As Lisa slips on the ring to prevent Lars Thorwald from discovering what she has found, she has, symbolically speaking, married him. And in that act, Jefferies is made to recognize another alternative to the possibilities of social involvement he has witnessed.

Observing Lisa and Jefferies' rear window communication, however, Thorwald, like Thor, the ancient god of thunder (Jefferies first observes his neighbor behaving suspiciously during a thundering downpour), takes action, threatening the very body of the observer-witness, an act that ends in Jefferies' defenestration, his literal fall—a fall not just *out* of his isolation and into the "here," but a falling *into* love and sexual being. The movie ends with Jefferies comfortably asleep (something he has been unable to do throughout much of the movie) aside Lisa who, reading an adventure-travel book, puts it aside to pick up a fashion magazine.

Given these perceptions about this movie, I see *Rear Window* now less as a study in cultural psychosis than as a comedy of social interrelationships, a comedic playing out of various sexual-social combinations that allow our "hero" to move from his child-like isolation to an adult social and sexual being.

Most of the perversity associated with this film, accordingly, seems to have less to do with the major character's careful observation of his neighbors— something he points out, that they also can do to him—than it does with a failure to recognize that the often frightening but essentially comic sexual and social encounters he watches are those of normal human beings—of us all.

Los Angeles, April 6, 2005

ERNEST LEHMAN (WRITER),
ALFRED HITCHCOCK (DIRECTOR)
NORTH BY NORTHWEST / 1959

Carey Grant and Eva Marie Saint in *North by Northwest*

Go West Young Man

While watching *North by Northwest* again the other night for the 50th time (I do not exaggerate, and probably I have seen this film more times than that) I tried to puzzle out why, at the highly judgmental age of 12, the year I first saw this film, I did not like it. The year before I had seen *Vertigo* at the same movie house and was completely enraptured by it. Certainly the latter film had confused me, made me even question whether it was an appropriate movie for someone of my age, but I had loved every moment of it, and sat through it twice. *Vertigo* is still my favorite Hitchcock film, but now, obviously, I find *North by Northwest* highly watchable and engaging.

While viewing it this time, it suddenly became apparent that it was the form that had put me off as a child. At the time, I had long been reading novels, and begun my passionate commitment to the theater, reading plays by Beckett, Albee, Ionesco and Genet. Given my literary experience—and ignoring the issue of whether or not I was able to truly comprehend these works—I could *understand* the psychological structure of *Vertigo*. Despite its strange double-helix narrative and its languorous cinematic love-affair with the city of San Francisco, I knew it was centered on the hero, Scottie. And the multiple meanderings and confusions of the plot were those of his mind. I may not have understood his obsessions—particularly his voyeurism—but I got the *idea* right off.

North by Northwest, on the other hand, was neither romance nor psychologically grounded fiction. The bond between Roger O. Thornhill and Eve Kendall involves no mysterious workings of the mind. They are immediately attracted to each other physically and proceed to do something about it—even if later, to protect herself, Eve must throw him to the wolves, so to speak. And he, in a reciprocal gesture, returns to her, even though he knows by that time that she is somehow involved in his intended death. No, this is most definitely not a "psychological thriller!" There is little about the mind in this film. Roger may not know *why* he is being mistaken for another man, but he knows *who* he is, and he is gradually told the true story behind it by the CIA (or whoever *they* may be). If information is withheld from the viewer it is not so that the character will gradually perceive and reveal it. We find out everything when he does; and we are simply told the information as if in a report. Eve, like her namesake, is purposely and necessarily duplicitous, engaged as she is with the both the serpent and the thorn-laden hill (the route out, so to speak) she must climb in order to escape her life of sin. Rather, the plot is driven by the mad linear movement of its characters on the run, from New York to Chicago and prairie environs, to Rapid City and on, finally, to the home of the symbol of American values: Mount Rushmore.

The structure is really quite a simple one, akin to the picaresque. Indeed, as in the traditional form, we meet our hero upon his metaphorical birth, so to speak, as he exits the dark cavern of the skyscraper office where he works as an advertising executive. It is hard to imagine the affable and handsome Roger as either an executive or a man who composes advertisements. Less important than his writing ads, he *is* a walking advertisement of American virility. "Do I look heavyish," he asks the secretary, who treats him as if she were his nanny. "Remind me to think thin." Like a child, Roger is completely selfish: his first action in the movie is to take over a cab from another would-be customer. And his dedication, like all children, is to his beloved and bemused mother. Indeed, it is his interruption of a business meeting to cable his mother that leads to his being kidnapped. As in a Charles Dickens fantasy, Roger is whisked away from home and family into a world of corporate castles (which he appropriately seems to know little of) and confused identities. After he receives the magic elixir (an overdose of bourbon) he escapes into the hands of the police, who like all authority in this kind of narrative, want only to lock him up and help to make things worse. After one last meeting with the disbelieving mother, he has no choice but to hit the road. And so he does, as adventure follows upon adventure until together the two lovers climb their thorny hill, the faces of their ideal. Roger even "dies," the way all picaros generally do. At least he *should* have died, were he in a more realist work. Hanging from the ledge of his monumental values, he is quite literally stomped out by the villain. But in such fantastic works, we all know, death is not a true option. As Northrup Frye has mentioned in his observations on the picaresque, although the picaro may die, he retains always the possibility of resurrection. Our villain is miraculously shot to death by the very authorities who have allowed Roger to fall into this position. It is also necessary for the sinful Eve to fall to her death; and she too, having "slipped," is left hanging in a position that seems quite impossible. We never see her actual salvation, only the simulated one, on the train, as the hero invites her into his bed.

To a self-satisfied twelve-year-old the simple actions of this child-like story seemed ridiculous.

Where was the depth of feeling and emotion? The high drama? The complexity of thought? If *Vertigo* was a masterpiece of modernist values, *North by Northwest* was an apparent throwback to what seemed to me then as a simplistic form—to the more linear structures that one might find in the early 17th and 18th century works and in the absurd coincidences of Dickens. We now recognize this return to older and hybrid forms as part of our postmodernist sensibility. And *Vertigo* seems, in contrast, to be a far more "old-fashioned" movie, a sort of angst-ridden portrayal of the existentialist man in the manner of writers like Sartre and Camus and artists such as Alberto Giacometti. One also now comprehends the comic genius of *North by Northwest* and enjoys the movie for the pure adventure of traversing the American landscape. And in this sense, the movie is (along with *Shadow of a Doubt* and *The Trouble with Harry*) Hitchcock's most American work. The next year the great director would return to more European forms in the Gothic horror tale told from the viewpoint of a the psychologically disturbed iconic figure of Norman Bates.

October 2003, Los Angeles

Reprinted from *The New Review of Literature*, III, NO. 1 (October 2005)

Applause, Applause

GEORGE CLOONEY AND GRANT HESLOV (WRITERS),
GEORGE CLOONEY (DIRECTOR)
GOOD NIGHT, AND GOOD LUCK / 2005

David Strathairn as Edward R. Murrow

Good Night, and Good Luck, George Clooney's and Grant Heslov's movie about Edward R. Murrow, is the kind of film that audiences always applaud. My companion, Howard, attended the movie twice before I took in a showing on a weekday afternoon, and at each performance, we concurred, the audience so responded.

Certainly the focus of this film—Edward R. Murrow's head-on attacks of Senator Joseph McCarthy and the House Committee for Un-American Activities, an act of great bravery on Murrow's and CBS's part—is worthy of audience appreciation. Murrow's reporting, his incisive appeal to his viewers that Americans ought to be able to encounter ideas that threatened their system without censorship or arrest, and his outright disdain for McCarthy's methods of innuendo and lies is well documented and in this film is represented through a noir-like dramatization of real events interspersed with actual television and film footage of the period. The world McCarthy and his committee had created is brilliantly presented by Clooney and cinematographer Robert Elswit in cinematic terms through extensive use of rack-focus camera shots and a blurring of the background in many scenes, along with jumpy, held-hand camera effects that recreate the sense of early television and suggest the psychological condition of people involved in a time when it was sometimes difficult to clearly see the broader picture of world politics and where even the tiniest of questionable political behavior might jeopardize one's career. W. H. Auden and others described the period as "The Age of Anxiety"; certainly it was a time when one nervous to do anything out of the ordinary—all of which Clooney and Heslov reiterate through several dramatic episodes, particularly in scenes revealing the hidden marriage of Joe and Shirley Wershba (played by Robert Downey, Jr. and Patricia Clarkson) [studio executives did not permit employees to be married] and the continual need for self-evaluation of personal sympathies or even relationships with those who might have had Communist connections [CBS news announcer Don Hollenbeck (played by Ray Wise) is attacked by newspaper columnists for having "pinko" associations, a slur which brings on his suicide; and, when Murrow (brilliantly played by David Strathairn) and Fred Friendly (played by Clooney himself) demand their staff tell them of any possible communist connections, one staff member suggests he should leave the team for having previously been married to a woman who had attended Communist

Party meetings before he met her]. In short, it was a time of deep paranoia that affected everyone.

On that fateful night in 1954, Murrow's "See It Now" broadcast crowned a series of events that would lead to the downfall of McCarthy and his years of destructive effects on the American psyche, effects that still have consequence in today's battles between the political left and far right. But if Murrow won the proverbial battle, he lost the "war," so to speak. A short year after that brave journalistic act (the movie unfortunately portrays it coming almost immediately after the McCarthy broadcast) CBS and its head William Paley (played here by Frank Langella) cancelled this regular news program, moving its diminished series of five shows to Sunday nights. And it is this fact that, it seems to me, is really the issue of this motion picture. Clooney and Heslov document the McCarthy attack effectively, but they have another, perhaps more far-reaching theme to present: the general decline of American journalism, and the rise of MTV-entertainment television and newspaper coverage. The movie begins and ends a few years after Murrow's famed show with a lecture he made to the American press about the ever-increasing lack of serious news coverage.

Accordingly, Clooney's film, although presented as a kind of realist drama, is more than that. It is a film of political commentary that continues to have important significance today. It is unfortunate that the film only suggests these issues—albeit quite forcibly. When one thinks about the declining coverage of serious events on US television, where local news stations now spend most of their time—at least in my city of Los Angeles—on car chases and disasters; when one perceives that even the half-hour of national news coverage reveals little about major international events; when one recognizes that journalists today often do not seem interested in pressing for the truth behind political statements and presidential edicts that are often promoted by implanted journalists, or that when they do question the issues, like Judith Miller, they connive and fabricate the truth; when one understands that most book sections across the country have been severely limited or suspended, or that as with the *New York Times Book Review* and *The Los Angeles Times Book Review* the book review editors have chosen, when it comes to literature, to refocus their attentions on more popular genres and best-selling publications; when one puts all of this and more into the context of Murrow's impassioned plea for more serious and complex reporting, one is perhaps made "nervous" again.

Do we as a populace know now when we're being lied to? Do we even recognize today that our news is incomplete—or worse—simply nonexistent? I am always depressed when I return home to my family in Iowa, where in the thin pages of the *Cedar Rapids Gazette*—just as in most smaller cities—the entire news coverage is presented in brief Associated Press notices? Yet my mother is convinced that she knows everything that's happening of importance in the world; "I keep up with the news," she proudly says.

Finally, it comes down to a societal and institutional disdain for Americans themselves, a feeling by a few who believe they hold knowledge (and often have no better grasp of it than anyone else) that the general populace cannot and will not assimilate complex information. A few years ago I had lunch with then-editor of the *Los Angeles Times Book Review* Sonja Bolle. When asked what books I was soon to publish on my Sun & Moon Press label, I replied that we had just published a translation by the French Oulipo writer, Raymond Queneau. "O, I love Queneau," she gushed, much to my surprise. "He's a wonderful writer. But, of course, we couldn't possibly do a review of his work!" "Why not?" I naively responded. "Oh, our readers couldn't understand a review about *his* literature. You know, most newspaper readers read at the sixth grade level."

I was appalled, not so much by the journalistic cliché we have all heard many times, but by the absolute misunderstanding, it seemed to me then and does yet today, of who her audience was. "Do you think," I asked, "that it is the least literate part of your audience who reads the book section? Why even have a book section if that's the case?" Inwardly I continued my argument: "We live in a very diverse time where readers seek out many different subjects and issues. And furthermore, I don't believe that any reader of a newspaper is a complete idiot. Don't you owe readers something more than your disdain?" I would have been talking to the wall.

Accordingly, I wonder, when those many audiences applaud Clooney's excellent film, just what it is that they are applauding: Murrow's bravery for attacking a bigot? Murrow's advocacy of a more serious journalism? Clooney's presentation of these issues? Or perhaps it is for all these reasons and more. I would like to think that in applauding *Good Night, and Good Luck* these audiences are simply asking to be treated as Murrow treated his, as intelligent adults.

Los Angeles, October 30, 2005

Reprinted from *The Green Integer Review,* No. 1 (January–February 2006)

The Prom King; Or, How I Learned You Can't Take It With You

MOSS HART AND GEORGE S. KAUFMAN
YOU CAN'T TAKE IT WITH YOU, DECEMBER 14, 1936,
BOOTH THEATRE, NEW YORK

MOSS HART AND GEORGE S. KAUFMAN
YOU CAN'T TAKE IT WITH YOU, PERFORMANCE AT
MARION HIGH SCHOOL GYMNASIUM, 1962

CLASS OF MARION, IOWA HIGH SCHOOL 1964, 25TH
REUNION, AUGUST 1989

Doug Reed, school annual photograph, 1962

In 1962, as a sophomore, I performed in a high school production in the small town of Marion, Iowa, of the great American comedy *You Can't Take It with You* by Moss Hart and George S. Kaufman. Even though this was just my second role, I knew from the way I was cast that I was destined to play small character parts: the year before I had played a child, Henry—the only black face to ever appear on our high school stage—in *Finian's Rainbow*; later, the same year as the Hart and Kaufman comedy, I appeared as Ado Annie's father in *Oklahoma!*; the next year I was a policeman in *Arsenic and Old Lace*.

Rehearsal for *You Can't Take It with You*, Marion High School, 1962. Doug Reed [second from the left], a young Mr. De Penna [far right]

This time round I actually had a few comic lines: I was Mr. De Penna, who, if I remember correctly, had one day paid a visit to the half-crazed Sycamore family and had never left. With the husband of the house, Paul, I supposedly built firecrackers in the basement and, from time to time—when she wasn't busy writing novels—modeled for the historical paintings of Paul's wife, Penny. Her father, who refused to pay taxes, ruled over the household that also included Paul and Penny's would-be ballet dancer daughter, Essie, and her husband Ed, an apprentice printer and xylophone player. Essie's ballet teacher, who daily showed up just before dinner, rounded out the insanity. Alice, the couple's other daughter, was evidently the only one not stricken by the family eccentricities; at curtain's rise, however, she had just fallen in love with her boss's son, and guess who was coming to dinner—the wealthy and quite pompous Kirbys, of course. Disaster was clearly in the air!

For me, a little disaster struck in a very different manner. During most of the rehearsals my parents were away in Europe, and my own slightly madcap grandmother was caring for us. I don't believe that the lack of parental authority, however, was responsible for the lecture given me by the director of the play. I had been giggling, quite loudly, backstage, and, after having been warned several times, had simply been unable to contain myself. I was at the age — how to put it nicely — of first sexual awareness, and a couple of other sophomores and I had been, well, "goosing" each other.

But perhaps the most exciting aspect of that evening for me (I'm certain it played a part in my rather bizarre behavior) was the very fact that I was acting as friend and peer in my small role as Mr. De Penna with one of the most beautiful males in the entire high school, Doug Reed, playing Paul. Doug was that year's football captain and soon-to-be-named King of the Prom! I have written elsewhere that I had gone through those years as an utter innocent, without any knowledge of my homosexuality. Given this recounting, however, I have now come to realize that I was a master of sublimation. For I knew, deep within, that I had an absolute crush on him. I recall staring at his picture over and over in the schoolbook annual at year's end. I had recently seen him, moreover, in all his glory! After having performed miserably in freshman athletics, I was dubbed by the coach — probably to please my superintendent ex-coach father — as the track and field "mascot," which meant that I followed the team on their various tours, helping to clean up the lockers. I'd had to hide my sudden erection upon seeing this splendid being in the raw.

That night, he must obviously have witnessed my sexual gropings. Now, as rehearsal came to an end, he asked if I wanted a ride home. Today, especially to adults, that may seem like a common enough question. But back then, as a child in 1962, it represented an earth-shattering event. The very thought that a senior could care enough about a sophomore to see him home, or that one of the most popular individuals in the entire school system would express such kindness to one of the least popular of figures was simply unthinkable. I sensed, even then, that there was something sexual in the air. Yes, I said, I would very much like that. My heart was nearly exploding with the excitement.

Now you must also know that, while I had just been accused of bad behavior, I was the most obedient of young men; I was what you would call a very "good kid." We had just driven a few blocks when Doug took out a cigarette. My eyes grew large with horror, as all of my father's moral imperatives kicked in. "I have to get out of the car," I stuttered. "If you're going to smoke, I have to get out of the car." And off I ran into the night. Was I in tears? I don't recall.

Years later I told this story, with wistful regret, to my friend Sam Eisenstein. "Well, it's a good thing you did what you did; you behaved in the only way you knew to protect yourself," observed Sam, "because if anything had happened, you wouldn't have been able to handle it." I knew he was right. I didn't have sex, with a male (or for that matter with a female), until I was a sophomore in college! But even as I spoke there as a sense of having somehow made a wrong decision, of having missed out on an important event in my life.

While I was attending college, I saw Doug once or twice on my visits home at the local library. Each time he was solicitous, polite, even interested in what I was doing in college. I wanted to suggest we have a drink, but was overwhelmed by his presence.

Another time, visiting my parents, I asked my brother, who was now the hometown football coach and had become friends with Doug's cousin Porter, my own age, what had become of Doug. My father, interrupting, muttered something about him being a bum. "Why is that?" I asked. "Oh, he just is," he responded. "He was dishonorably discharged from the military or something like that." Nobody seemed to know any details, but my suspicions were further aroused. I never saw Doug again, but I have always wondered, was he truly gay? How terribly lonely he must have been.

In 1989, more out of curiosity than any real caring or interest, I decided to attend my 25th class reunion. I had not really liked my classmates, and, in fact, had not even graduated with them, since I had spent my senior year abroad. One finds oneself from time to time, however, stupidly sentimental: I accepted the invitation—besides, it was time for another family visit.

I had been thin for much of my youth, had had something close to a ballet dancer's physique, if not a dancer's agility (which I came to realize studying for a few months at the Joffrey company in New York). But time had changed things, and I was now somewhat overweight. I had just dyed my graying hair back to its natural blond. "It's the best I can do," I said to the mirror. I heard my parents in the other room, changing clothes as well. "What are you doing?" I called into their bedroom. "Getting ready," they innocently replied. "Do you mean you're going too?" "We were invited!" I was flabbergasted. All those years of my childhood, I had attended every school event with my parents in tow—it was, after all, part of my father's administrative responsibilities. And now, at the age of forty-one, it was happening all over again! "Please stay home," I begged. Off we all three went!

Everyone has stories about class reunions, save those who are very wise and do not attend. For me, the evening was one of the worst of my life. Despite my added weight, I was one of the thinnest males in attendance. The first person to come up to me had been the center of the football team during the tortuous freshman year when my father insisted I go out for the game. I played center for the second-string team (there were only two teams), and each time I hiked the ball, this large bison of a being immediately descended upon me. "Remember when I used to jump you every time you hiked the ball?" he asked me right off. Yes, I recalled; but why had *he*? After all these years? Had it been that special in his life? "Every time you hiked the ball," he laughed, "you lifted your head." Oh?

The second person to come over had been the brightest girl in our class, a rather intelligent woman I had always thought. This evening, she served as the hostess to the event, speaking a kind of bimbo blather; her husband could be found in the men's room telling stories about her stupidity.

I quickly found the bar and began busily drinking when suddenly dinner was announced. The bar closed! Alcohol, evidently, was not to be imbibed during the activity of eating. Milk and iced tea—neither of which I can tolerate—were served in its stead. Groups quickly captured the various tables. The farm girls sat, where they always had, at the fringes. In the very center of the room the group which had seen themselves as the "smart set"—made up of the 1964 Prom King and Queen, as well as two other women from the same year who, after the Prom King's divorce from the Queen, had also married him—hunkered together as if not a day had passed. The choral director—that very same drama coach who'd lectured me that special evening long ago—invited me to sing. "No," I quickly blushed, "I no longer sing." I sat with the losers. As each member of the room recounted his or her current vocation, it quickly became apparent that the vast majority of my classmates had become insurance adjusters. I was ready to escape.

Then, suddenly, across from me, there was Porter Reed. I'd always liked Porter; he wasn't as handsome as his elder cousin, but there was a family resemblance, and, like his cousin, there was a sort of gentle kindness in his voice. I swallowed a piece of grisly roast, and went straight to the heart: "Porter, can you tell me what has become of your cousin Doug?"

Porter paled. "Oh, you haven't heard."

"Heard what?"

"Well, you know Doug as very athletic; he always

kept his body lean. He'd become something of an alcoholic and had begun to gain a little weight. One day he took a rifle to his head and shot it off!"

I stood. Across the way were the only two humans I could recognize in the room—my parents. "We should go," I said.

Los Angeles, September 2004

Reprinted from *The New Review of Literature*, II, NO. 2 (April 2005).

How ROTC Saved My Life —and Granted a Transcendent Revelation

The Dow Chemical protests at the University of Wisconsin, Madison occurred in February 1967.

These protests were some of the earliest political actions against the war in Viet Nam on university campuses during the decade, and would foretell many of the violent encounters between students, faculty, local police, and the military over the next few years.

In 1966 and 1967, as a freshman and sophomore at the University of Wisconsin (first Milwaukee and then Madison), I participated—incredibly to those who know me well—in the Reserve Officers' Training Corps (ROTC). One must remember that during those years the United States was at war (an undeclared war, but a war nonetheless) in Viet Nam. My father reasoned, quite logically, that if for some inexplicable reason I was drafted out of the university or if the war were to last—as it did—after my graduation year, I would be better off as an officer.

Still an obedient son in those years, I, accordingly, took a weekly course in ROTC, first in the Army unit and then in the Air Force. I certainly didn't enjoy the activities, which to my way of thinking were a bit like having to attend physical education classes. Yet we did little, actually, that could be described as physical. Mostly we marched in straight lines of three or four individuals, while someone shouted nearly indecipherable commands. Sometimes even I was asked to command these little squadrons, which I did by trying to imitate the inchoate barks of our older sergeant. I was fairly good at imitation—evidently. Besides, I'd done more marching, in even straighter lines, during the years of high school marching band!

One day we were handed rifles and asked to take them apart. I was terrified, but I was able somehow to dismantle the thing; but when I was asked to put it back together again, I was completely stymied. After an interminable time, during which everyone else had managed to transform the pieces back into devices for killing, I had no choice but to hand in the parts. Nothing was said.

When I transferred to Madison, the marching seemed to stop. Maybe they reasoned that we had learned that task. Now we began to take courses—although I don't recall a single thing I was to have learned. All I do remember is that one day we were told to stay away from the protests against the Dow Chemical Company (who produced the napalm that had destroyed so many lives in southeast Asia) currently taking place on campus. [The February 1967 protests lasted for two days, during which time 17 students were arrested, and the Chancellor, blockaded in his offices, demanded their release and ultimately barred organizations such as Dow from interviewing on campus.] "You might get hit in the head," warned our instructor, "and if you were to become unconscious, all of your chances of flying would come to an end."

I hadn't heard of the protests, and immediately after class rushed out to observe them. It was a bit boring—at least while I was in attendance—as students and faculty peacefully marched holding picket signs bearing photographs of napalmed Vietnamese children round and round the Chemistry compound.

A week later, I was called to the Commandant's office; I didn't know we had a Commandant! Had someone seen me at the protests? I was terrified. In the back of my mind, however, I suspected that this demand might have something to do with the battery of tests we had recently been administered. I hated tests with multiple-choice answers. I was particularly bad—a near-idiot in fact—when it came to math and science questions. I was once told that if, instead of attempting to answer the questions posed on the Iowa Test of Basic Skills in those areas, I had simply chosen to pencil in the boxes at random, I would likely gain a higher score than I achieved by trying to make sense of the questions asked.

But now, in college, I was an honors student, and by shirking most of my science and math requirements, had kept a high grade point average. Indeed, ROTC wanted me! This test, I ascertained, had found me out!

The Commandant asked me to sit, and quite sympathetically inquired whether I was feeling better.

Fortunately, I didn't dare to respond as I was tempted: "Better than what?"

"Because you must have been quite ill last week, when you took our tests?"

In the years since this incident, I am sorry to report, I have learned to be less honest than I was on that particular morning: "No, I wasn't sick. Not that I recall."

"Well, I'm afraid you must have been, given the results. I mean," he continued, apologetically, "you were quite excellent in your language skills and in history. But…well, I don't know how to put this…. we have never had anyone score lower in their skills in science and math."

I was strangely relieved. "Well," I perked up, "I can assure you I wasn't ill. That's just what happens to me when it comes to math. I've always done horribly in math and science — except for Algebra. I once got a B in that!"

He was still quite sympathetic about my apparent delusion. "Well...I still presume you weren't feeling well. I mean, you're an honors student, for God's sake!"

"Yes, but I've never been good at math, and so — even though I enjoy the ideas surrounding it — I'm not good at science either. I just don't understand it, no matter how hard I try."

"You can't become an officer without it, I'm afraid. How would you fly an airplane? But — well, we don't usually do this — in fact, we never have — but, I'm willing, in your particular case, to — well....we'll have some of our senior students tutor you, and we'll be willing to allow you, as a big exception, to take the test over again."

Today, I realize that this poor man, stuck as a military representative in the most unforgiving of outposts outside of Berkeley, was speaking to me in a kind of code. He was trying to tell me, without coming out and saying it, that he and the mysterious upperclassmen of which he spoke, were going to pump me with the answers.

I was still an innocent, however, and all I could see ahead were long hours of being drilled with imponderable calculations and strings of meaningless numbers cornered into what I perceived as a division sign with an attached check mark. The radical root of so and so is such and such. I knew that no matter how I might desire it, my mind would never take it all in.

"I believe you can do it," he said, in a voice that sounded as lovingly positive and sadly misled as my father's, "and I'm going to give you that chance — if you want it!"

"Well," I squirmed, "I've just never been able to assimilate numbers."

"Or, perhaps, if that becomes your decision — I'll give you a day to ponder this — it may be that ROTC is not right for you...."

"What!" my inner mind protested, was I being told that I didn't belong? I'd never been told that about anything — except perhaps for fraternities, which I had no inclination at all to join, and sports, in which I had no interest. Wasn't I officer material? My uncle was, after all, a three-star general at the time, well on his way to a fourth star!

"If you choose not to take this opportunity," he continued, "I suggest you might see a psychiatrist — about your mental block regarding math."

"Mental block!" I nearly cried out loud. "Psychiatrist!" No one in my family had ever even seen a psychiatrist—or talked about one. It was an inconceivable subject, absolutely something not even to be considered unless experiencing a nervous breakdown—and no one in my family of nearly 100 first cousins had ever come close to that. I didn't have a mental block! I was simply stupid when it came to math! What was this man *talking* about?

"Yes," I meekly agreed, "what you suggest about tutoring me is probably the thing I should do."

"But I want you to think it over," he kindly spoke, sounding more and more like my insistently kind and completely wrong-headed father. "Let me know by tomorrow, if you can."

I carried a mountain of confusion with me back into my little room in a boarding house across from the University of Wisconsin football stadium. For some reason, I recall pacing in circles in a room I did not inhabit—the room of an overweight and—reportedly—wealthy Filipino who seemed to sleep night and day without attending classes. I wonder why I picture myself in that slightly larger room as opposed to my little corner cell. Perhaps it was the gravity of the situation that demanded—at least in my imagination—more space. All I recall about my actions was the circling. I circled and circled, seemingly unable to focus on the issue at hand. Circled and circled—both in body and head. Why was I taking this all so seriously? I wondered even then. It seemed, suddenly, such a very important decision—a matter somehow of life and death.

Then something within me snapped. Was I having a nervous breakdown after all? No, I felt good, my mind felt free. And everything seemed to make sense. I saw my life so very clearly for the first time. I remember it now, another circle around the room while I spoke to myself out loud: "You do not believe in the military, do you? You don't like the war in Viet Nam. You aren't even a Republican! You don't believe in your parents' political values." I was amazed. Yes, it was true. I was a Democrat, maybe even a radical, certainly a Socialist. When had all that happened?

I circled another time, and more came out of my astonished mouth: "You don't believe in God. You've been going to church just to sing in the chorus, but you haven't liked the ceremony for years. You don't have your parents' faith, so why do you pretend to yourself that you believe in religion like you do? This has got to stop!"

What was happening to me? I was somewhat frightened, but I was even more relieved.

One more time round the room was necessary. My voice was quavering by this time, afraid of the words issuing from it: "And you're not ever going to get married. You don't like sex with women. You're gay. Admit it, you're gay!"

I stopped. I was floating, I felt as light as air. So this was what so many writers—Faulkner, Welty, Woolf—had written about. I had just had, I suddenly understood, a very special experience. I had undergone a vision, a transcendent vision. I would never be the same. I lay down on the bed.

A little later I rose and went downstairs to call my father. He was terribly disappointed with my decision to drop out of ROTC. I think he cried; perhaps I did. I didn't tell him about anything else. I too had learned how not to say what I really meant.

A few days later, I visited the university psychiatrist. I was nervous.

"What seems to be the problem?" he asked.

I could hardly speak, but finally came out with it in a trembling voice, "I think I'm gay."

"What makes you think so?"

"Oh I just feel it. I know."

"Have you had sexual relations with other boys or men?"

"No," I answered, slightly embarrassed about the truth.

You must remember that it was 1967, and I was attending one of the most liberal campuses in the country.

"Why don't you try it, and see if it's something you like—if you really are gay," he calmly suggested.

And I did.

Los Angeles to New York, May 12, 2005

Reprinted from *The Golden Handcuffs Review*, NO. 6 (Winter–Spring 2005–2006)

Creative Writing 458, or
How I Learned to Write Immorally

The creative writing course (whose actual number I do not recall) was given by Isaac B Singer at Madison, Wisconsin in 1967. My visits with Singer in New York occurred in late 1968 and 1969.

Isaac B. Singer

When I was a sophomore at the University of Wisconsin, I determined to take a creative writing course that was primarily for upper-level students. I had previously had a creative writing course — a rather dismal experience with a little-known novelist — at the university in Milwaukee. But it was not really the writing that led me to want to enroll in the course, but the man who was teaching it, the Yiddish writer Isaac B. Singer. I was surprised and delighted to hear that he was teaching at Wisconsin, although I never bothered to ask why or how had he come to be there. Although the great story-teller and novelist was already well-known — I'd read several of his books — he was still not exactly a household name, and I suppose he was happy to have the money. Perhaps he had a close friend on the faculty, or…well, the idea of this urban-based legend sloshing through the cold snow across the Madison campus was amusing to me. He'd required a story for entry into the course, and the word had just come down, I was selected!

As I recall, we met class every other week. Those few classes were an absolute delight for me. It's not that I learned how to write — Singer's primary lesson to young writers was to write about place, to write out the experience of upbringing—something which, blame my itinerancy, I couldn't quite respond to. But he was wonderful in the classroom, full of funny and wise sayings and little stories concerning everything from his place of birth in Poland, to remembrances of how he had come to the US, the brother of an already famous author, and been absolutely terrified to publish anything. He had, so he claimed, burned the galleys of his first book, canceling its publication. When some of the students—all older than I—probed him about other contemporary Jewish writers such as Saul Bellow and Philip Roth, the corner of Singer's eyes glistened with a slightly naughty and possibly malicious intensity as he explained how he was no fan of their work—something with which I was in complete agreement. I loved each of our sessions.

However, as clever as he was in telling stories, Singer was not very wise when it came to selecting my fellow students. To me the university was filled in those days with exciting students from all over the country. But for some reason—perhaps because these students *had* written about where they lived—most of my classmates were from Wisconsin, and a duller, less sophisticated group could not be imagined. They were disinterested in Singer's marvelous musings, and regularly interrupted with protests or their own rather insignificant observations. One day, a young woman suddenly burst out in the middle of one of Singer's marvelous retellings, "O look! Look!" as she pointed to the window. Singer slowly shuffled over the window scrutinizing the sunset: "Oh, yes, it's doing that same thing again," he answered in his heavy Yiddish accent. I was disgusted by the interruption.

Little was I to imagine that that simple-mindedness and country-bumpkin stupidity would soon be directed against me! It was time to read our stories to the rest of the class. Singer called my name, and I quickly stood up and went to the front of the room, nervous, hurried. Singer had to tell me to slow down several times before I caught on. Finally, I read the story at a more leisurely pace. There was a deep silence.

"Well," coached Singer. "What do you people think?"

Eventually, a senior raised his hand. "I think that this is the worst story I have ever heard," he exploded. "It's immoral," interrupted another. "It's—well, you can't write about things like that!"

"Like what?" Singer asked, seemingly nonplussed. "How is this immoral?"

"Yes," I uttered within my head. "How can this story be immoral?" I couldn't comprehend. What were they talking about?

Before going any further, perhaps I should recount the subject of my story, based on real-life experience. That year I was working in the university Admissions office—I had even been given a key to the Administration building so that I could do my work late at night (to this day, I can't believe my innocence in not recognizing that I had been offered incredible trust, that had I been a political activist, I could have brought the University to its knees!). In any event, I met there a middle-aged woman, who befriended me. She always reminded me, a little, of Shirley Booth, or, later, of Shelly Winters—a kind of overweight, sad being, who had, evidently, a son by a former husband. One night she asked me if I'd be willing to "baby sit" the child. I had often taken care of children throughout high school, so I readily agreed. I arrived at the appointed time, and was introduced to her son, whom today we would describe as a hyperactive child. I played with him for while in his bedroom, finally getting him into his pajamas and into bed, while his mother, presumably, finished dressing for her evening date. But when I approached the kitchen, there she sat in the same bathrobe in which she had greeted me.

"Would you like some coffee," she asked, "or a little brandy?" Brandy suited me better—although I had just begun to drink. We talked. We talked some more. I checked on her son, returned. And we talked. It was apparent that she was not at all intending to leave. Although I was quite innocent in those days, I wasn't an utter idiot. I realized that she had invited me over for intentions that lay outside the care of her young son. I felt as if I were playing a role in a movie based on a play by Robert Anderson, William Inge, or — more probably — Tennessee Williams: *Tea and Sympathy*, *Come Back, Little Sheba*, *A Streetcar Named Desire*. And I was clearly the object of desire, even if she cloaked it with the verbal ramblings of a lonely housewife. Finally, I told her — despite her protestations — that I had to go home, and I stumbled off into the night.

My story was simply a recounting of that event. Nothing sexual had happened in reality and nothing happened in the tale, even if the intent of the character had been that something might. I was suddenly being described as an immoral author for writing about a quite innocent event. It wouldn't be the last time I would be described as writing immoral literature, but, as a young man, unable to realize the absurdities of my culture, I was stupefied. So, apparently, was Isaac Singer. We bonded, a bit, after this incident. Still today, I have his signature in all of his books published to that date, one addressed to my pseudonym of the period.

The next year, when I temporarily left the university to live in New York, I met with Singer on at least two occasions. The first time, we met at the deli/cafeteria where he usually ate—Singer was vegetarian. We talked about his new story, just published in *The New Yorker*, about that same cafeteria, and about a writer we both loved, Knut Hamsun. As we walked back to his nearby apartment, Singer asked me which Hamsun novel I most loved. *Mysteries* was my immediate response. He too felt that that was Hamsun's best work, and offered to give me his original edition. Unfortunately, when he went to look for it, he couldn't find it. What a treasure it would have been, representing two of my favorite authors in a single object.

On a second visit, knowing of his interest in strange phenomena, I reported a story I had read in the newspaper: scientists had evidently been doing an experiment with plants, hooking them up (quite inexplicably) to lie detectors. When they threatened the plant (whoever had thought to do so? I remember wondering), it apparently went haywire, producing readings on the lie detectors that were equivalent to a hyper-emotional state.

When I told Singer this tale, he put down his water glass. "I don't believe a potato can think," he quietly replied. "I don't think plants are emotional

77

beings.....Besides, if it were to be true, what *would* I eat?"

For several years after these events, I was afraid to write another story. And when I returned to writing fiction, I tried to make my stories as "immoral" as I possibly could.

Los Angeles, May 16, 2005

Nine Nights In New York

The First Night: 252 72nd Streeet

Columbia University

Upon completing my junior year of college at the University of Wisconsin, I was nearly desperate to get to New York City. It so happened that a co-worker in the Admissions Office and her husband were planning to drive there at the close of the semester, and they asked me did I want to join them. I readily accepted.

The trip, as I remember it, was a long one, since we took a northern route through Indiana and Ohio, and moved yet further north into New York State so that we might stop by her sister's house in Skaneateles. My friend's sister, it so happened, had married the architect-developer James Wilson Rouse (who had built many projects including the

Faneuil Hall Marketplace; later he'd design the planned community of Columbia, Maryland and developments in the harbor area of Baltimore.) Like many of the houses in Skaneateles, their home was a mansion, where we stayed the night and part of the next day. I recall a good discussion with Rouse about urban development.

Later that day we drove down to New York City, staying with her husband's brother and wife in a small apartment on 72nd Street.

I had determined to spend at least the summer in New York, but had failed to report this information to my own family and had made no provisions for a place to live or even given any thought to how I might survive in the metropolis without money. I can't even imagine, today, my complete lack of fear and knowledge of the consequences. I just presumed something would come up — and indeed it did.

My friend's relatives knew of an apartment belonging to a puppeteer, now on tour, that stood empty on Horatio Street in the Village, where the next day I was duly shipped off. I stayed there for about a week before I moved in to the Sloane House YMCA (it would be nearly a decade before The Village People gave their corroborating advice) and ultimately, I shared an apartment in Jackson Heights with someone I'd met in that august institution.

I began temporary employment with NBC, moving boxes of old records for two days. That was followed by a typist job with a Swiss manufacturing company in the Chrysler Building. They were so impressed with my typing and—I guess—my personality, that after several weeks they tried to hire me as a salesman; but I could never comprehend what kind of machinery they produced, and even after attending a meeting in lower Manhattan with someone from the company attempting to describe what I would be selling, I could make no sense of it. Perhaps these were newer models of "Miss Emmy," the monstrous computer of *Desk Set*.

Soon after, I moved to Steuben Glassware, where I was asked to create a scrapbook of all the glassware that had been given as gifts to foreign dignitaries by the Presidents of the United States. That took me through several weeks before, following a tip I'd received from my previous employer in Wisconsin, I applied for a job at Columbia University, where I was immediately appointed Assistant Director of Protocol. The head of Protocol—Mrs. Torbert—and I planned for the dinners and activities surrounding several events, including award ceremonies such as the Bancroft and Pulitzer Prizes. We were also in charge of organizing and scheduling events for the Board of Trustees of the University. At these occasions I was responsible for advising the President of the University of everyone's name and the sequence of his activities; often I had to dance with guests and faculty wives. That year the Bancroft Prize was awarded to James Watson and Francis Crick.

Meanwhile, I was enjoying the open sexuality of New York, and on almost any night I could be found at the gay bars in the Village. I often started at the renowned Julius' (dining on one of their famous hamburgers) before trekking over to Stonewall and heading further West to a bar near the trucking docks whose name I can't recall, but which, late at night was the site of backroom orgies. I was quite attractive and thin in those days, and generally had picked up someone before the long trek to the docks.

This little history will tell you that some time had passed since my embarking at 72nd Street. And I had still failed to inform my poor parents that I was in New York! Today, it seems unbelievably cruel of me to have behaved so irresponsibly. The idea that my parents would be terrified by my unexplained absence never seemed to reach the synapses of my brain. My only excuse now is that I was young, and like many young men, utterly selfish. Life was exciting—things had worked out, despite my lack of planning! And I had no intentions of interrupting my adventures with a call home!

One evening during my tour of the various bars, I met a young man who, following the usual pattern after hearing how far away I lived suggested we go up to his place. We entered the subway or perhaps we took a taxi, and headed up town. "I know this street," I blurted out as we exited either subway station or taxicab; "It's 72nd Street." The boy smiled.

I was more than a bit startled when he entered the same apartment building in which lived the relatives of my Wisconsin friends. I was even more overwhelmed by coincidence when he soon thereafter opened the door to the very apartment where they had lived. "I just moved here a few months ago," he mysteriously reported.

"Yes," I said, "because I knew the former tenants."

"You did? How strange."

"Yes. Indeed it is."

That was the end of it—the strange event—so I thought. We had sex, and I was preparing to leave—or perhaps to stay for the night. I can't remember. Then the telephone rang. It was for me, reported my new friend.

"What?"

"They asked for you."

"But no one knows I'm here," I responded, shaking a bit as I picked up the receiver.

It was my mother! Where was I? Where had I been? She'd had to call the University to find out that I'd gone away to New York with some friends, and they had told her that I'd stayed the first night with their relatives. My mother had called here now to find out if they knew where I might have gone. Why hadn't I told them? Was I coming home? Was I quitting school? She was in tears. My father was crying in the background out of a mix of what I now recognize as horror and relief.

I don't think I said much. I just told them that I was staying on in New York, and wasn't at all planning to come home just yet. But I promised I would keep in touch.

I don't recall whether I stayed for the night or not. I probably slept in that bed in the master bedroom of the apartment in which I'd spent my first New York night sleeping on the living room couch. For I now realized now that whatever choices I made, there could be no escape. Fate or God—whatever one called destiny—was clearly on the side of my parents. Or perhaps it was on my side, since I soon realized I had been ready to be found.

Los Angeles, June 7, 2005

Reprinted from *The Golden Handcuffs Review*, NO. 8 (Winter–Spring 2007)

The Second Night: Party Going

My short year of living in New York in 1969 was a very lonely one, and I made few close friends. I *had* met a young man, John Diserio, at Julius', the gay bar in the Village, and I was invited several times to his apartment, often with other of his friends, most of whom were several years older than I. They were all quite intrigued with me, in part because of my obvious youth and innocence, but also because of my knowledge of arcane information which seemed to suggest experiences that belied my age. They were all interested in theater, and I was a whiz concerning Broadway musicals. I recall them testing me again and again on the names of shows and their songs; one question in particular stands out: John or one of his friends asked me, "What musical contained the song "That's Good Enough for Me." He sang a few bars. I had probably only heard the piece once, in a booth at the local record store, but I guessed right off: *How Now, Dow Jones?* They were flabbergasted.

Another time, when John was temporarily out of a job, he invited me to lunch. On the way to the restaurant and through most of our meal John bemoaned the fact that he'd still not found a new position; he was getting nervous since his savings were beginning to run out. "You know, I have a woman friend, Mia, she's been a friend for years—but I seldom see here. Yet every time I have difficulties she suddenly contacts me. I don't even know where she is these days, or I'd call her. She's one of those rare individuals who's a bit psychic. She'd tell me what to do, and I'd do it."

We finished lunch and left the restaurant, beginning to cross a nearby park. Suddenly John stopped in his tracks and pointed to a woman approaching us. "There she is! That's Mia!" John introduced us, and Mia took my hand: "You're a Gemini," she said. "Yes, I am," I admitted.

I left the two of them to discuss old times and the solution to John's problems.

I mention this friend and his group because it must have been one of them who invited me to a party in Brooklyn. I determined not to go, but when the time came, I dressed and got on the subway. I'd never been to Brooklyn, and as we came to the tip of Manhattan, I asked someone where I should get off to find the address I'd carefully written down. He told me, but a man standing nearby who'd overheard our conversation disagreed with his instructions. A woman chimed in, another man, and another. It was hilarious as they all bickered with one another, each trying to drown out the others' voices. It was a scene, in short, right out of a Broadway musical. New Yorkers so desperately want to be friendly they even argue over it!

I was more confused than ever, but I did get off at some juncture and evidently found the right place.

Much of that evening is lost in my memory—it was, after all, 35 years ago. I do remember there being a great many rooms in this apartment, each filled with young gay men drinking, kissing, and fondling, in the first stages of what promised to become what today would be called an "orgy." In that time and place it probably wouldn't have turned out that way. There may have been sex at this event, but if so it was quite discrete, two or possibly three men at a time in one corner or in one room, others scattered about the place.

Disinterested in the action in the room in which I stood, I began to wander. I took in the kitchen, the living room, a couple of bedrooms, and finally entered a third bedroom where several boys sat around a figure lying on the floor. The scene reminded me, a bit, of something out of Fellini, a Bhishma-like character out of *Juliet of the Spirits*, and, in that sense, quite surreal. Who was the figure on the floor and why were all these young men hovering about him?

I moved forward, but still couldn't get a glimpse of the figure as I remained a few feet away. After what seemed like a long while waiting for the young men to finish whatever it was they were doing, I moved forward until I stood directly over the hunkering boys and the focus of their attentions. It was Og! The Og of the University of Wisconsin production of *Finian's Rainbow* in which I'd been a singer-dancer. I don't recall his real name, just that he'd played the leprechaun in the Harburg-Lane musical. He was definitely cute, but in an odd sort of way: he wasn't diminutive, but he had a strangely large head that sat upon his smaller frame. His lips curled up at strange angles, and his eyes were so dark that they drew one into staring at this face in wonderment.

"Hello," I said.

"Why, hello," he answered back, "We know one another, don't we?" His apparent suitors all turned toward me.

"Yes, we were together at Wisconsin. You're Og."

I can't imagine what the others thought I was talking about, and I don't now recall whether I joined them in what appeared to be almost worshipful group sex act. I only remember leaving the party soon after. There was no sign at the affair of John Diserio or any of his friends, so perhaps I had not been invited by any of them. Who had invited me? Perhaps no one. When I left the apartment I saw that it was not the number I had written on that paper in my pocket.

My life has seemed always to be made up of a series of coincidental or accidental interlinking events.

I took the subway up to Columbus Circle, deciding, despite the late hour and my slightly drunken condition, to walk the rest of the way up to my apartment on 111th Street. Now I knew how to behave like a New Yorker. I generally was quite aware of my surroundings and any individuals lurking nearby. But that night my movements were more like those of a wanderer, a tourist taking in the sights. I walked slower than I usually did and avoided the glare of any faces I encountered. Besides, it was difficult to see anything at 1:00 a.m.

As I approached my street and turned, I heard the sound of feet behind me. I sped up a little, hurrying toward my apartment. An arm grabbed me and a knife was placed at my neck. The attacker pulled me into the outer lobby of the building next to the one in which I lived and quickly demanded my money. I don't know if it was because I had had a few drinks or whether I just naturally might behave this way, but I was not frightened as much as outraged. I had just cashed my paycheck and all the money (money which had to carry me through the next month) was in my pocket.

"Now listen," I assertively spoke, as the robber took by billfold from my pocket, "you can have some of that, but you *have* to leave me some. I haven't got anything else!"

He paused for a second before demanding I shut up.

"I need some money!" I pleaded. He handed the empty wallet back.

At that very moment a woman passed, and he turned to see if she might be heading in our direction. As he turned back I saw he was nervous, even shaking a bit, and suddenly I was also afraid. "Drop your pants!" he commanded.

"What?" I shouted.

"Drop your pants!"

I presume he simply wanted to make certain that I wouldn't follow his escape, but that morning, the way he looked at me with his fearful insistence, I wasn't certain of anything. "Now you robbed me, get! You got my money and I'm not giving you anything else. Get out of here!" I exploded.

He did.

After a few seconds, I left, entering the building next door. I didn't even call the police. I'd simply been a statistic, I felt. That night I'd been the perfect prey.

Los Angeles, April 7, 2006

The Third Night:
Cupid's Arrow Gone Astray

Me in 1970, shortly after New York

I remember the bar as being quite far downtown, but I can't imagine what might have led me to be at such a remove from my usual Village haunts. It was a fairy typical evening, in any event, and now it was getting late without anyone having chosen me as a sexual partner. As some boys had told me in the past, I often looked "too serious," and they'd been afraid to approach me; I'd worked hard to develop a friendly smile. Perhaps it just wasn't my night, I admitted, as

I turned to leave. Suddenly directly in front of me was a handsome blond with a truly dazzling smile and smoky blue eyes. He leaned forward to give me a kiss.

Richard Charmatz, who worked as a curator at the American Museum of Natural History, was older than most of the young men with whom I'd gone home. He reminded me of the kind of boys of the mid-1950s to which I had been secretly attracted, an attraction that I represented to myself as terror—a fear of their cockiness, their girls, their cars. In their blue denims and carefully combed shocks of hair, they signified to me everything that I was not—and had been educated to be different from. I fell in love with Dick, I suspect, because he so clearly reminded me of the kind of male I had unknowingly desired throughout my childhood.

For Dick, I was, in turn, a bit like a trophy he could display to his group of friends: a cute young boy who was also fairly clever. He showed me off, accordingly, at parties and other events over the next few weeks, as a relationship developed between us. I recall, for example, attending a rock concert of The Who, performing songs from their "rock opera" *Tommy*, with him and a few others in New Jersey, a contingent of gay men who, in those days, had "camp" names and delivered up *bons mots* in exaggerated accents at their weekly –sometimes nightly—gatherings.

Dick was also a product of the 1950s in other ways—his politics were virulently conservative as opposed to my recently radicalized beliefs, a difference so vast that we sometimes had shouting matches. Dick, accordingly, did not at all approve of my living quarters so close to Harlem at 111th Street. His stylish apartment was on East End Avenue, and he was determined to find a place for me nearer to the East Side. Ultimately, I shared an apartment with several young men—including his former lover, a boy I truly disliked. Four or five of us living there attempted to find a kind of group employment, and one or two of them actually began a typing service named—after my suggestion—"Hunt and Peck."

I visited Dick nearly every night. But over several weeks, I began to feel that his delight in me was fading. One day he simply announced that he'd have to stop seeing me: a friend with whom he'd promised to "try out" a relationship had returned from England. In fact, he admitted, "I had thought it was him when I kissed you the first time we met."

I left his apartment with tears welling up in my eyes. It was a grey day, and I hadn't the energy even to return to the collective apartment. I went to a nearby phone booth and called my parents. In a day or so they wired me the money to return home.

Richard Charmatz

Vance George

Back in Madison, Wisconsin, where I landed a week or two later, the university choral director, Vance George—with whom I'd had several sexual episodes during my college years—invited me to join him and opera student Pat Dickson, a large Italian girl with an infectiously joyful personality, in a house they were caring for. It was the home of Paul Badura-Skoda and his wife. Austrian pianist Badura-Skoda, with over 200 recordings to his name, had already worked with conductors such as Wilhelm Furtwängler, Herbert von Karajan, George Szell, Zubin Mehta, and numerous others; his wife was a noted musicologist. I gather they were in Europe for a few weeks, and Vance and Pat were temporarily serving as caretakers for their home. The three of us shared the huge master bedroom bed, snuggling up to one another, giggling and kissing like grade-schoolers in a kind of innocent love-fest that perfectly suited my now slightly bruised ego. Pat cooked Italian sausages, hand-stuffed by her farm-dwelling brothers, and served it with fresh fennel for dinner—some of the most delicious food I'd tasted. We talked of love, music, dance, and art.

After a few days, I found a new apartment and began attending classes again. A few weeks after, on February 4, 1970, friends and I attended the first gay liberation meeting at the University of Wisconsin.

There I met Howard Fox, with whom I have lived for some 36 years since that night.

Vance is now the Director of the San Francisco Symphony Chorus, and is recognized as one of the leading international choral conductors; occasionally he visits us in Los Angeles, when he attends the Grammy Awards for which he and his Chorus have often been nominated (and won). Pat reportedly joined some religious order; she always had a quality about her of some sacred goddess. Staying with us for a few days in Washington, D.C., she stopped by the Islamic Mosque where workers were evidently retiling the walls; when Pat appeared in the doorway they ran toward her, presenting her with an arm full of the older tiles. We have one of those holy relics in our kitchen today.

Dick and his companion visited Howard and me years later in Washington, D.C. I had the feeling that the relationship was not working out. He cornered me in our kitchen, but his kiss was less gentle — and far less passionate — than the one I received by mistake that first night.

Los Angeles, April 17, 2006

The Fourth Night: At George Plimpton's

The offices of *The Paris Review,*
downstairs from George Plimpton's apartment

I believe it was the last year I attended the Small
Press Book Fair. I don't remember the date, but it
must have been in 1979 or 1980. The Fair—which
had been in various venues over the years, including
New York University and somewhere below the Port
Authority—was located that year in the 7th Regiment
Armory on Park Avenue and 67th Street. There was
the usual mix of small literary press publishers—few
of us very enthusiastic about the event. Audiences

were thin, if I remember correctly, and the whole event wasn't what you'd call a great success.

In the late afternoon, as we all grew more and more exhausted manning our tables, the military (evidently the Seventh Regiment), which had obviously been out on maneuvers all day, decided to return. They drove their jeeps and tanks into the Armory, encircling the small press tables. But rather than simply driving into the space and parking their various vehicles, they kept the engines running, with the result that the huge space was soon filled with exhaust fumes. Many of us—both customers and publishers—began to feel light-headed, and had to escape to the outside. It was clearly intentional, since, as we headed to the doors, we could see the grins and chuckles of the soldiers. Ultimately, they turned their engines off, but by that time it was too late to continue the fair, and we returned to the exhaust-filled space only to pack up our books and retreat.

I recall walking down the street with other participants, filled with outrage and disgust for the whole event. "Whoever organized this event ought to be shot," someone complained. "Perhaps they already had been by the army boys so smug about their distaste for our literariness," I quipped. Several of us went for drinks, and I found myself sitting beside Vicki Hudspith, who had just interviewed me (or would soon interview me) in *The Poetry Project Newsletter*. At the time, I believe, Vicki was the Director of the artistic board of the Poetry Project and over the years she has continued to write poetry, and direct events and plays, including John Ashbery's *The Heroes*. She was (and probably still is) a beautiful woman; I'd heard that she had had a background as a fashion model—but that may simply be gossip.

In any event, several of us (I believe we were joined by Maureen Owen and others), were having an enjoyable late afternoon conversation. I had been invited to a party that evening at George Plimpton's house, and, as the hour approached, I suggested Vicki and others join me. We arrived at Plimpton's a bit drunk. But then most of the party-goers who had already arrived were also somewhat tipsy, so it didn't seem to matter; Plimpton, it was announced, was in an airplane overhead, unable to land because of bad weather. So the party really had nothing special to commend it; without the famed host, it could have been anyone's house.

Finding it a bit difficult to stand without swaying, I found a comfortable chair, and Vicki came over to join me. "Where did you grow up?" she asked, which I remember feeling, coming out of nowhere as it had, was a strange question. "In a basement," I answered, a bit glib in my intoxication.

"Really?"

"Really. I moved to the basement at a very early age, and, except at dinners, seldom spoke to the rest of my family."

"That's strange," she replied, seating herself on the floor next to my feet. "Because I grew up in a basement too!"

"What a coincidence."

"I'm sorry that I kept calling you Dave."

"I didn't know you had."

"Because I went to school with a Dave, a Dave Messerli. So I kept calling you Dave back at the bar."

"That's odd, because I have a brother named David, a bit older than you. Where'd you go to school?"

"I went to school far away, in Cedar Falls. Northern Iowa State University. Ever heard of it?"

"My brother didn't go there. He went to the University of Iowa. But my sister, Pat, went there. She must be your age."

"That's strange. You're from Iowa?"

"Yes."

"Where?"

"Cedar Rapids."

"Cedar Rapids! I'm from Cedar Rapids!"

"You are? Then, you'll know where I'm really from: Marion, a suburb."

"I'm from Marion!"

"You lived in the basement?"

"Yes."

We'd grown up just a few blocks from each other. It now seemed, as we sat in that house (with its own renowned basement wherein *The Paris Review* was produced) up on 72nd Street (the same street, although on the other side of town, where I'd spent my first night in the city) that Vicki and I were enacting the scene from *On the Town*, when Gabey and Ivy discover they were both from Meadowville, Indiana! But I was no longer surprised. I now realized that my life would always strangely coincide with art.

Los Angeles, June 9, 2005

The Fifth Night:
The Relation of My Imprisonment

Lewis Warsh

Russell Banks

Bernadette Mayer

Perhaps my worst night in New York centered around a very pleasant event, a book party to celebrate the publication by Sun & Moon Press of Russell Banks's fiction *The Relation of My Imprisonment*. That book was an important one for the press, bringing us our first national attention for publishing a living writer, including a review in *The New York Times Book Review*. With the publication of that book and Djuna Barnes' *Smoke and Other Early Stories* (which had previously received national acclaim) I was contacted by a sales representative for New York and the Middle Atlantic states, Bill Whitaker, who later helped to find other sales representatives and brought the press to a more professional level. I might add that the book was also important for Russell, since the attention he received for this short fiction helped to generate interest for his novel of the following year, *Continental Divide*, which gained him international stature.

We had planned a book party for late in the season — it must have November or December — a few months after the book had appeared. I was staying, as I often did, at Charles Bernstein's and Susan Bee's apartment on Amsterdam Avenue, a two story-affair in which life was a bit like living — as Susan herself described it — in steerage. I generally stayed in Susan's studio, which lay a floor below their living quarters. I slept on a small pallet on the floor, but I enjoyed their company so much, I never minded—and I was only in my mid 30s in those days, easily able to endure whatever pains might be attached.

I had probably arrived in New York, as I usually did, a few days earlier to purchase the hors d'oeuvres, supply the bar and arrange for a restaurant meal for a smaller gathering after. Russell had convinced the owner of a small gallery in the Village to serve as the location for the event.

I recall arising that morning in good spirits: there was just enough chill in the air to please me. I should tell you, right from the start, that I do not like coats! For most of the winters I lived in Washington, D.C., Philadelphia, and New York I survived without one, wearing only a sports coat and scarf. I like the cold and have a natural stamina for it.

I left the Bernsteins' coatless that morning and puttered around the Village—East and West—for much of the day, making sure the restaurant was prepared for us and, if habit is any indication, probably scouting out special book finds at the Strand for a few hours. By mid-afternoon it had begun to snow, and by dusk there were small banks of snow accumulating. I returned to the Bernsteins' who had decided to drive—an activity in which they seldom engage in the city—to the event. We arrived fashionably early and, after meeting the owner of the gallery, I put my host-and-publisher smile upon my face. People began to arrive. I soon realized, however, as the evening wore on, that I wasn't feeling at all well. My back hurt, my legs were giving out. My face felt the slight tinge I always feel when a fever threatens. By the end of the party I was feeling quite dreadful, as if I'd fallen down a flight of stairs. I had the dinner still ahead.

I'd told Russell whom I had invited to dinner, a small group, Lewis Warsh and Bernadette Mayer—who'd first published the work in their magazine—and friends such as Paul Auster, Charles and Susan (who'd declined), Michael Brownstein, and, of course, Russell's wife. By the time we began the short walk to the restaurant I noted several others tagging along. I had prepared for this, but it worried me that, as we moved through the streets, the group appeared to be growing in size. Leslie Scalapino happened to have been in town, and so I invited her to join us. Novelist Mark Mirsky had suddenly appeared out of nowhere. A number of others trailed behind. We found the restaurant and settled into the large horseshoe shaped booth, adding a few chairs to the outer rim. Suddenly I realized I was sitting between Leslie and Bernadette.

Leslie is now a dear friend, and I truly love her. But at the time I did not know her well and her intensity, a quality which I now admire in her, made me uneasy. She is, I have since perceived, a slightly shy person given to silence between somewhat dramatic and always intelligent statements. I am quite talkative, certainly gregarious — in short, a bit afraid of silence. It was the long pauses between her comments that frightened me. I felt as if in each of those long draws of her breath she was trying to comprehend the fast flow of information coming from my lips and thoroughly evaluating it.

Bernadette can also be a truly enjoyable person. But she and Lewis, long married, had just separated, and that evening she was — to put it nicely — psychologically on edge. Bernadette was emotionally disturbed by the fact that the waiters wore formal attire, and she was quite ill at ease with the fact that I had involved her in a dining experience quite outside of her usual bent. She told me so several times, repeating her consternation in my right ear, while Leslie intensely spoke into my left.

It may be, of course, that at another time I would have found both of their behaviors quite ordinary, but I was now running a high fever, and suddenly I felt that the stairs from which I'd metaphorically fallen had actually been a cliff.

Mark Mirksy, whom I later published, is a wonderful storyteller, someone who is truly gifted. But that night he had decided, apparently, to tell—over and over so it seemed to me in my feverish condition—tales, with a strongly Yiddish flavor, about Minsk and Pinsk. Russell is also a wonderful storyteller and so too is Lewis—indeed the room was filled with them, and each began to tell their tales.

I remember little else—not even what we were served or how I had paid the bill or had returned to the Bernstein apartment. I only recall, as I put my body upon the floor, that if I felt as I then did in the morning I would seek out the emergency room of a local hospital.

Morning came. I had made an appointment to see an artist who wanted to do a cover for Len Jenkin's forthcoming novel *New Jerusalem*. I intended to call him, bowing out of our appointment, since my condition had not at all improved, but I had only his address. Charles and Susan were terrified when I appeared, and I thought perhaps when this person saw me, he might release me to go my way. So I showed up for the appointment, explaining that I was quite ill. He was delighted to see me, seeming oblivious to my pallor and began to display work, after which he insisted we go to lunch. I tried to demur, but I was too exhausted and simply followed, dazed, unable to eat anything or even to insist upon my right to disappear.

Again, I have little memory of what happened after that. I must have found my way to the train station because I recall Howard meeting me in Washington and, upon seeing me and hearing my whimpers, whisking me away to bed.

I lay in that bed, nearly unconscious, in alternating fits of fever and chill, for an entire week before I fully awoke. Howard—who seldom had experienced illness—had not comprehended the seriousness of my condition, although even he had decided one day that my extremely high fever required the attention of a doctor. The weather, however, had gotten worse; we were suffering a cold snap and blizzard conditions, and he was afraid that if he took me out of the house I might become even more ill. Perhaps he was right.

A few days later, I telephoned Paul Auster to talk about his upcoming publications "You know," he said, "I got sick at that party, the one at the restaurant. I went home and fell into coma. The doctor diagnosed pneumonia. I'm just now getting back on my feet."

"You too?" I responded.

Los Angeles, July 10, 2005

The Sixth Night: A Poetry Reading

Perhaps we were all at a reading—if so, it must have been at the Ear Inn. Or perhaps we just planned to meet there to go out together later—although I don't believe we went elsewhere. But there we were—James Sherry, Charles Bernstein, Bruce Andrews and I—all in a bar I believe was called Lucy's, a little dive that attracted a wide range of lesbians, gay boys, and older Chicano men. I'd been there once before with James, and found it such an unusual place, I'd probably been the one to suggest it this time round.

We were, as usual, already intensely speaking about the subject of poetry. I have no idea what we were saying, probably something about voice or audience or the need for a more intensely controlled disjunctiveness.... We were enjoying ourselves over drinks, talking the way we—four of the central figures of what many people then called "Language" poetry—usually talk about poetic issues that mattered terribly to us.

I had also been noticing the handsome elderly man in the corner, who was obviously attentively listening to us speak. We did our best to ignore him. Fortunately, there were few others in the place.

Suddenly, we heard a noise coming from the corner. We paused, heard nothing, and continued our speculations.

Whan that Aprill, with his shoures soote
The droghte of March hath perced to the roote
And bathed every veyne in swich licour,
Of which vertu engendred is the flour;

The words were whispered, almost a murmur. We turned our heads. The man in the corner begin to speak just a little more loudly.

Whan Zephirus eek with his sweete breeth
Inspired hath in every holt and heeth
The tender croppes, and the yonge soone
Hath in the Ram his halfe cours yronne,

"Yes, Chaucer," said Charles.
"Oh, so you *do* recognize it," said the gentleman in a Southern accent. He continued, now speaking in at a fairly normal level of voice:

And smale foweles maken melodye,
That slepen al the nyght with open eye-
(So priketh hem Nature in hir corages);

Charles continued for two lines:

Thanne longen folk to goon on pilgrimages
And palmers for to seken straunge strondes

"You were talking about poetry, weren't you?" asked the elderly gentleman.

"Yes," I responded, "contemporary poetry."

"Because I couldn't understand a word of anything you said."

Bruce laughed. "We must sound strange. We were talking about *our* poetry," he responded

"Your poetry?" the man seemed a bit surprised. "I thought maybe you were a bunch of professors."

Charles laughed. "I'm sure we sound like that, but we're not—a bunch of professors. Some of us teach...but..."

"I like poetry," said the man at the other end of the bar, a Chicano of middle age. "My wife writes poetry."

"She does?" I asked.

"Well, she tries to," the Chicano quickly corrected himself. "I like it."

We all smiled.

"I was just trying to get your attention, to talk about *real* poetry," said the Southern gentlemen.

"And our poetry isn't real?" James asked.

"It doesn't sound like it," said the gentleman.

"I like *real* poetry," said the other man.

"What makes you think our poetry isn't *real*, whatever that might mean?" I asked.

"I bet your poetry doesn't even rhyme."

"Does some times," answered Charles.

We all turned back to return to our own conversation, but a pall had overcome us, and we could no longer speak without great self-consciousness. Instead, we broke into laughter, the four of us, the Southern gentleman, the Chicano man, even the bartender.

To ferne halwes, kowthe in sundry londes;
And specially from every shires ende
Of Engelond, to Caunterbury they wende,
The hooly blissful martir for to seke
That hem hath holpen, whan that they were seeke.

"Let us be off to Canterbury then," I said as we made our way out.

Los Angeles, June 5, 2005

The Seventh Night: Coincidence

"My life has seemed always to be made up of a series of coincidental or accidental, interlinking events," I wrote, if you recall, about the second of these ongoing New York nights. I know for some people it will be difficult to believe in such a series of coincidences; all I can say to such suspecting folks is that I have not knowingly fabricated or exaggerated any of the events of this book. And I don't think I could even have imagined them.

On one of my many trips to New York, I arrived at Kennedy International Airport and decided that instead of taking the taxi into town, as I usually did, I'd take the bus. The trip was an eventful one. At some point in the freeway tie-ups the driver decided to make his way through the surface streets of Queens; but unlike some of the taxis who make similar detours, this driver seemed to be drifting increasingly inland from the freeway. As his meanderings became more and more noticeable, a group of riders, growing alarmed, began a quiet mutiny which, as it became apparent that the driver was now lost, grew into a shouting match. "Let me out, here!" insisted a couple of the passengers as we arrived at the dead end of a mean-looking Jackson Heights street. The driver was growing nervous and more and more flustered.

As I write elsewhere, there is something about the missionary (and perhaps the schoolmarm) in me, and I just couldn't resist: I stood up before the entire bus and demanded quiet. "He's lost," I noted the obvious, "but I can assure you that you wouldn't want to get out at this corner! Just let him find his way back to the freeway."

At that point I turned to the driver and quietly suggested that he make a left turn, then a right, another left, etc., and before we knew it the freeway was in sight. I had lived one summer in Jackson Heights, but I had never driven its streets. Moreover, I'm often not accurate when it comes to directions — although in every city, in every county I've visited, I have been stopped and asked for directions, so perhaps I exude confidence, even if I am not the perfect navigator. In any event, we ultimately found ourselves in Manhattan — two hours after leaving the airport!

I quickly took a taxi to my hotel, the Summit, now Loew's Midtown Hotel. I must have appeared a bit haggard after my adventures on the bus, for the man at the desk asked if I might like an executive suite at the same price as a regular room. I assured him that that would be fine.

I showered, redressed, and went downstairs to seek out a good restaurant. Since I knew the West Side better, I waited for a taxi. The doorman asked if I wouldn't mind riding in a limousine for the same price as a taxi ride across town. No, I didn't mind. The limo, which could easily have seated five or six individuals, was a gleaming machine that the driver had evidently just purchased and for which he was eager to develop a clientele.

Along the way, I decided to stop by J & B's, a rather seedy venue across from what used to be called "Needle Park" on Broadway. My limo pulled up to the door of this dilapidated drinking establishment and I grandly exited. It must have looked surreal. The driver handed me his card, which read "Doug's limousine." Would I have any further need of it while I was in town? he queried.

Today at J & B's they demand "cash only," obviously distrusting even their down and out regular customers. I like the place, however, because it's one of the few city locations where, as long as you buy a drink, you can stay for hours writing at a table. At the time I was working on my fiction, *Letters from Hanusse*, a book that took me over twenty-five years to complete.

I was concentrating on a scene which was to appear early in the book. The narrator, living in New York (a native Hanussean who spends much of the fiction in Paris) was expressing his fears of the city:

I have always feared the unimaginable. That the building in which I lay myself down each evening might one night just crumble into pieces upon my sleeping head. It's possible, the building is old, badly in need of repairs. It's not an earthquake I imagine, it's simply *my* building and its inevitable collapse.

I looked up for further inspiration, and across the way from my table noticed two young women deep in conversation. While pausing with pen in air, I overhead one of these women say, "This may seem strange, but you know what I most fear?" "What?" the other asked. "That someday—and this will sound silly—my building will just fall down, that it will collapse."

Had I spoken aloud what I'd just written? I wondered in alarm. No, I realized, I wasn't even whispering, which I sometimes do when I write. Could they have read my writing from their position at the neighboring table? No, we were several feet apart; I couldn't even read the title of a book that sat before one of the young woman who had just uttered these frightening words, and I was facing them. Had they read my mind? I didn't stay to find out, and I later cut that passage from the final manuscript. It was too close to reality, I decided.

I hurried up the street a ways and dived into a local eatery. Peace. What was happening? Why had the hotel man given me such a large room? Why had the limousine driver described his automobile as mine? How could that woman have repeated aloud what I had just imagined on the page?

At the bar I ordered a drink and some soup, which the tender quickly delivered up.

For some reason I can't explain I have the habit of engaging bartenders—and bar patrons—in conversation. Perhaps I inherited this behavioral pattern from my father, who often embarrassed me as a child by chatting with nearly everyone at any café or restaurant we might enter.

"So what do you do when you're not bartending?" I asked as he paused for a moment between mixing drinks.

"I hope to be in the theater," he immediately responded.

"Dumb question," I quipped. "You and every other bartender in town."

He was not at all offended. "Yeah, but I don't want to act. I want to direct."

"Really."

"And what I'd like to do is create a theater company to perform the kind of plays I want to direct."

I couldn't resist. "And what kind of plays would you like to direct?"

"A group of new playwrights."

"Such as…."

"O, you wouldn't know them. They're younger playwrights with just a few plays to their names."

"I know something of theater," I boasted. "Try me."

He served up an order and came back to our conversation. "Well, I was in Austin and stopped into this bookstore where I discovered this marvelous anthology of plays—they were great plays by younger writers. Plays I'd like to see produced."

"Yeah?" I goaded.

"The book was called *Theater of Wonders*," he went on, lighting up. "And they were truly wonders in every sense."

"The book was published by Sun & Moon Press?"

"Yes," he responded, slightly taken aback.

"Edited by Mac Wellman?"

"You know it?"

"I am the publisher of that book. I'm Sun & Moon Press."

I gave him my card. "I don't believe it."

I'd finished my soup and downed the rest of my drink. "Good luck," I said upon paying him.

New York, May 7, 2006

The Eighth Night: La Dolce Vita

Paul Vangelisti

In 1991, Luigi Ballerini, then a professor in the Italian Department of New York University, organized a conference of contemporary Italian poetry which included several major Italian and American poets. Among the Italians were Edoardo Cacciatore, Alfredo Giuliani, Biagio Cepollaro and the late Paolo Volponi and Amelia Rosselli. Americans included Charles Bernstein, Bruce Andrews, Lyn Hejinian, Jerome Rothenberg, Paul Vangelisti and Elaine Equi. Numerous critics such as Marjorie Perloff were also in attendance. I won't describe the event, since my experiences with the Italians at the conference, particularly with Giuliani and Rosselli, might be better placed in a future piece about Italian poetry. Let us just say that the conference itself was an unusually tense experience, particularly given the outspokenness of several of the Americans. A cultural war was brewing by the conference's end.

Afterwards, most participants quickly left. But Paul Vangelisti and I—both from Los Angeles—were forced to stay on in order catch planes out the next day. When Paul asked where we might have dinner, I suggested a nearby Italian restaurant with the improbable name *La Dolce Vita*, where some of the participants (Rothenberg, Andrews, Perloff, Ballerini, and I, among others) had eaten the night before. So off Paul and I went.

The restaurant was fairly good, but I no longer remember anything I ate. Paul and I always enjoy one another's company, particularly when we get a few drinks into our systems. For Paul tells wonderful stories—and I, so I feel, don't do badly myself. But this evening our center of attention was elsewhere. Our waiter, a very short, Truman Capote-sized man, was quite clearly attracted to me. It was obvious that he was gay, and that night he was more than obsequious in his attentions. When Paul suggested that we finish dinner off with a *grappa*, we ordered the least expensive — and the only affordable one — we could find on the list. But our waiter insisted that that wouldn't at all do. "I'll bring you another one," he announced. The other *grappas* on the menu were priced from $40.00 to $100.00 per drink! But that didn't seem to stop him, as he brought us first one incredibly good drink, then another, and another — each one priced higher than the previous and all, evidently, on the house. Paul had clearly noticed his attentions, and now, as the waiter hovered over us, monitoring our reactions to each sip, Paul began — as he is prone to in such ludicrous situations — to giggle. His is an infectious giggle, and I too — as the alcohol kicked in — could not resist laughing. Our waiter overlooked our now nearly raucous behavior, and paid even closer attention to us. "Are you going to be here tomorrow night?" he queried. "Because that's my night off."

"No," I attempted to answer with a straight face. "I won't be in the city tomorrow."

"Oh, dear," he replied. "I have an even better *grappa* for you to taste," and off he went to get the even pricier bottle. Paul was almost on the floor with laughter by this time.

I had to go to the bathroom, and when I opened the door to return to the table, there was the waiter standing guard. "I get off at 12:00," he reported.

What could I say? I quickly returned to the table and swallowed the new *grappa* he had deposited there. Paul was giggling uncontrollably.

"We must go," I insisted, afraid that if we stayed any longer I might explode with the howl I had been holding in.

We put down our money, and looked up into the face of a clearly chagrined, almost tearful being. I felt bad, but I needed to escape.

The way out of this restaurant was through a long narrow bar featuring swivel stools that left just enough room for patrons to pass behind. Paul led as we pushed our bodies through the gauntlet of stool backs as quickly as we could. Suddenly, a hand came out and rudely pulled me into a chair. It belonged to a quite beautiful woman, a long-haired blonde who had determined, for some reason, that I was to sit next to her. I called out to the escaping Paul, who turned back in complete astonishment.

"You have to have a drink!" my captor insisted.

"No, I've already had too many drinks," I retorted. "I have to go."

"No, you have to sit!" demanded my jailor, pulling me down into the chair again.

Paul was performing a little dance in a new fit of laughter.

"I've got to go," I insisted, trying to rise from the stool once more. But again, she pulled me back into its surrounding protection.

"Not until you have a drink."

"I've got to go," I said, nearly jumping to the floor and running toward to door. Paul followed, and we exploded into the street.

What magic had I possessed? My pheromones must have been particularly pungent that night. Paul and I were now consumed by an absolute hilarity. Our laughter was contagious, for others, passing by, began also to laugh.

We dove into a nearby cab. It was apparent, given the evening we had just experienced that it would be no use for either of us to return to our own hotels—at least not yet. Since we were in the Village, I suggested we speed off to another part of town, the Upper West Side, an area I knew well. Things will be calmer there, I thought to myself. And off we went.

I don't believe I had ever before been to the bar we entered on Broadway and 82nd Street, at least I didn't recognize its interior, but it seemed a suitable place in which to calm down our now overactive libidos. We bellied up to the bar, but all the liquor I had consumed had filled my bladder. Order me a gin and tonic, I said on my way to the john. I had gone just a few feet before I heard the bartender's voice ask Paul what he'd like to drink. Paul told him. "And what will your publisher have to drink?" he calmly queried. Paul fell from the bar stool in utter disbelief. And I returned just to help him up.

Los Angeles, June 4, 2005

The Ninth Night: My Broadway Hit

Jerome Lawrence

Shortly after the night of my mother's surprise telephone call to 72nd Street in 1969, I bought a ticket to a preview performance of the Broadway musical *Dear World*. This musical, based on Jean Giraudoux's *The Madwoman of Chaillot*, was written by the Broadway veteran libretto and playwrighting-team Jerome Lawrence and Robert E. Lee. The music was by Jerry Herman, and, like *Mame*, Herman's musical based on their *Auntie Mame*, starred Angela Lansbury; the supporting cast included Jane Connell and Milo O'Shea. Despite my empty bank account (indeed I had no bank account in New York), I had saved up just enough to purchase this ticket, and I was excited about the prospect of seeing what promised to be another Broadway hit!

As I left the lobby of the Mark Hellinger Theatre and walked a half block to Broadway I reached into my pocket to examine my newly acquired treasure. But the pocket was empty. I tried another, felt in my back pocket, jammed my hands quickly into the deeper pockets of my overcoat. No ticket! How could I have lost it in a journey of a half block? I had, after all, held the ticket in my hands in the theater lobby. Where had I put it? Had it fallen out of my pocket? I retraced my steps without finding it, returning home—I was now living in a Columbia University apartment on 111th Street almost facing the Cathedral of St. John the Divine—spiritually depressed.

It was mid-December and I'd bought this ticket as a kind of Christmas gift to myself. Now with the holiday quickly approaching, I had nothing to do, nowhere to go. For some inexplicable reason, I dressed (shabbily I am certain) for the theater on the evening for which I'd purchased the ticket and arrived at the theater just as the crowd moved forward to find its seats. I moved with it, stopping to speak confidentially to one of the ticket-takers. "Honey, you see that woman over there. Go talk to her," the ticket-taker said. I went over to the woman she pointed out—her name apparently being Dorothy, since that was what her blouse announced—and abashedly tried to explain my presence: "I'm sorry to bother you, and I wouldn't be bothering you, but I bought a ticket for this performance and lost it. Is there anything I can do? I'm telling you the truth."

"Of course you are, honey. I believe you. Come with me," she said, taking my arm and leading me up into the balcony. "Here's a good seat," she gestured to a chair that was probably in a much better location than the one for which I had originally paid.

"Thank you," I called out as she turned to back to the lobby. "Thank you."

Unfortunately, the musical was not very good—was certainly not a "hit." The work was far too intimate to survive the canyons of the Hellinger theater, and the sets by the acclaimed Oliver Smith seemed to be located in some grand palace rather than the supposedly dilapidated home of the Countess Aurelia, the madwoman of Chaillot. Jerry Lawrence later admitted to me that Joe Layton, the director, and Jerry Herman had insisted upon the larger-than-life production. But it wasn't the kind of musical, with its dark expressionist elements, that could sustain the brassy theatricalism of Herman's more populist work.

In any event, I did get to see my play. Don't let any one ever tell you New Yorkers are always rude and inconsiderate!

But this story is not meant to portray another of my coincidence-haunted New York nights. I suspect the kindness shown me was not the first or only example of Dorothy's empathy for her patrons. I mention this event only as prelude to an evening that truly was a Broadway—*my* Broadway—hit, even though it didn't occur in a regulation theater.

In 1992 I hosted a book party in celebrating the publication of a novel by William Fadiman. Fadiman was a salty Hollywood figure—he'd been Dore Schary's assistant at MGM studios when Schary was chief of production and, later, president of that studio. Several Hollywood celebrities, accordingly, were in attendance, as well as William's more-famous brother, Clifton, who after a long stint on NBC's "Information Please," had been the senior judge for the Book-of-the-Month Club, later editor in chief for the publishing house, Simon & Schuster, and *The New Yorker* book editor. It was there I met Jerome Lawrence.

Throughout my childhood, I had admired the Lawrence and Lee team. Auntie Mame—along with Rosalind Russell, who will always *be* Mame to me—was one of my very favorite characters of the stage and movies and *Inherit the Wind* was among the American plays I most treasured. Howard and I'd also seen their *The Night Thoreau Spent in Jail* (not one of my favorites) in an Arena Stage production in Washington, D.C. Jerry and I quickly became friends, and few weeks later I visited him at his legendary Malibu home filled with theater memorabilia—a grandly modern house that tragically burned to the ground during the canyon fires of 1993 shortly after the events I am about to describe.

We spoke of the possibility of my reprinting some of Jerry's and Robert E. Lee's plays. But first—there was often a carrot attached to my friendships with elderly men—might I take a look at a novel he had just completed? The book, *A Golden Circle*—a novel about theater based on several of the figures he'd known—was not a particularly brilliant novel, and was certainly not the kind of fiction Sun & Moon Press generally published. Yet it was an enjoyable read, a gentle and loving tribute that might attract any slightly sentimentally inclined lover of the theater. I agreed to publish it.

The book appeared in early 1993, and I determined to promote it later that year with a party at the Algonquin Hotel in New York. We settled on a night in May, when Jerry's friends would be in town, he suggested, to see plays before voting for the Tony Awards. He handed me a long list of invitees, to whom my assistant Diana and I mailed out formal invitations. It included nearly everyone of theater fame!

For my visit, I took the Thurber suite in the hotel. We'd rented the Oak Room, and Jerry had quietly planned the performances. I had ordered hors d'oeuvres and liquor (a full bar), arranged for a photographer, and planned on serving as Master of Ceremonies and general host.

After a few nervous rehearsals—singer Michael Feinstein does not like mornings—we were ready for the evening event. Among the attendees were caricaturist Al Hirschfeld and his wife; restaurateur Vincent Sardi; conductor Michael Tilson Thomas; poet Charles Bernstein with his artist wife, Susan Bee; lyricists and composers John Kander, Fred Ebb, Jerry Bock, and E. Y. Harburg; actors Michael York, Marian Seldes and Jan Handzlik (the original Patrick Dennis in the Broadway production of *Auntie Mame*); and playwrights Robert Anderson and Elmer Rice, as well as younger dramatists I'd invited such as Mac Wellman, John Steppling (coincidentally stopping in New York on his way back to Los Angeles), Len Jenkin, Jeffrey Jones, and numerous others.

Pianist/singer Bobby Short begin the performance part of the evening during the cocktail hour, and when the guests were soon after seated, Michael Feinstein took over the piano and sang a song from *Dear World*. I took up the mike, explaining who I was and how delighted I was to see all my old friends—even though I'd never actually met them. But they were *old friends*, I explained, from my childhood, a time in which I memorized the Burns-Mantle playbooks, read their plays, and purchased their recordings—even before we'd owned a record player! Now I was overjoyed to meet them in the flesh.

Jerry Herman took over the piano with Michael Feinstein singing a medley of Broadway songs, and before we knew it, E. Y. Harburg had been drafted to sing "Old Devil Moon" from his *Finian's Rainbow* (the musical that has reappeared time and again in my life). A reading from Lawrence's novel by Tony Randall, Jane Alexander, and E. G. Marshall was next on the bill. Paula Robison followed with a flute solo, and Michael Feinstein returned to the piano to sing more songs, several of the audience members joining in.

On the plane to New York, I had sat next to an elegantly dressed woman who talked a great deal about the theater, and on a whim, I had invited her to the affair. As the evening came to a close, she came over to me and whispered into my ear: "This is the best thing on Broadway! I couldn't have imagined such an evening possible." Neither could I.

Los Angeles, June 7, 2005

Martha Scott, Jerry Lawrence, and Burgess Meredith reading from *A Golden Circle*.

Carol Channing with purse upon her head.

Soon after this New York theatrical event, we had a smaller west coast celebration for Jerry's book at Books & Company in Malibu. At this affair, actors Martha Scott and Burgess Meredith, along with Jerry and his young "secretary" Will, read passages from the book. In the audience Carol Channing sat throughout the performance with her purse perched atop her head, evidently for protection from the afternoon sun. I'd long before witnessed her performances of Hello, Dolly! *in two different cities, Chicago and Washington, D.C.*

New York, May 5, 2006

Making Things Difficult:

An interview Between Charles Bernstein & Douglas Messerli

BERNSTEIN: Many of your poems are written, as you put it, "after" other poems. Can you talk about the ways you approach writing "after" poems both in English and also other languages?

MESSERLI: When I first began speaking about my poems being "after," I was thinking of the method I use to create many of my poems, namely "collage." In numerous works, sometimes just to get the poem started, I look at the writing of other poets, and play with their word combinations; the first two words of each line, odd word couplings I find particularly generative. By and large, I never use the work of just one poet, but numerous writers, some whom I've actually never read. The eye discovers what it wants to in each poem, and that, in turn, creates a series of associations, leaps, imaginations, narrative interpolations, that allow for the flow of my own poetry. As someone (Jen Hofer, I think) once described me, I'm sort like the "grand recycler" of poets, a kind of repository of bits and pieces of the thousands of poems by Americans that get published each year. I don't know if I can really claim that role, but I don't mind its implications — after all, I am one of the major publishers and anthologists of poetry in the US, and I probably read more poetry each year than anyone in this county — particularly given the demands of my grand (ultimately 50 volume) series of PIP (Project for Innovative Poetry) anthologies. So, in that sense, I encounter thousands of poems which, given the methods I've described, bring bits and pieces of a great many poems into a new kind of existence "after" the works of others.

When I came to *After*, however, the idea of that word had shifted. What I had begun to realize is that in reading so much poetry, and in working through many of those poems to stimulate my own writing, I had indeed been changed somehow by the process. Particularly in relation to the so-called translations I had done, my poetry had been transformed, become richer and denser, so I thought. Although I took high school Spanish, college French, and learned boarding-school Norwegian, along with a smattering of German, I don't really have a command of any language except English. So I didn't want to claim the role of being a "translator," a figure I hold in high esteem. I called my "translations," accordingly, writing *after*. The word was useful since it suggested both the effects of that poetry I had translated, and some of the methods I had used in bringing my own poetry to life. I alternated poems in that volume that were translated or written "after," with poems of my *own*—whatever that might mean—that had been affected, in some respects, by my engagement with the poems in other languages.

I might conjecture—now that I've just recalled a specific incident—that my poetry may have always had a quality about it that linked it to translation. When I first began writing, I joined a group of Washington, D.C. poets (Doug Lang, Phyllis Rosenzweig, Lynne Dreyer, Tina Darragh, Peter Inman, Anselm Hollo [a great translator of the Finnish], Bernard Welt, Diane Ward, and Joan Retallack, among them) for weekly readings of our poetry. One evening, after hearing me read, Welt said of my work: "Your poetry sounds like you've written it in another language and then translated it into English." At the time, I was reading very little poetry in translation.

These "after" poems, moreover, had also come after a long spell of what I think of as very American poems represented in *Dinner on the Lawn, Some Distance, River to Rivet: A Manifesto* and *Maxims from My Mother's Milk/Hymns to Him*—the last, given its imbedded American clichés, slang, puns, and other rhetorical expressions, is about as American as you can get. *After* was clearly more influenced by international work. So it represented a kind of new turn, "after" the heavy concentrations of wit and punning I had become known for. My next undertaking, *Bow Down*, went one step further, in that, since I knew I was writing for an Italian audience—the book was published by an Italian publisher and translated into Italian—I wanted to further push the idea of writing after. So this time, I chose the works of Italian poets in translation, and wrote "through" these writers (using many of processes I've described above) and, simultaneously, wrote with collages of the Los Angeles American-Italian artist John Baldessari in mind. Accordingly, there was a kind of layering in *Bow Down*, a combination of image and word, that, when put into the context of my own associations, became something very different from, but was strongly influenced by the Italian. It's strange to think of these works—which had come out of Italian through English—as being translated "back" into Italian. I am sure that to the Italians it had very little relationship to the original language. But in English the Italian came through. I'd again been influenced by another culture, had had the benefit of coming "after."

More recently, considering all the performative works I've written, and the long, yet unpublished manuscript *Between* — for which I wrote through the works of poet friends and then, sending the pieces to them, asked them, in turn, to write through my work as a whole or back through the poem I'd just written — I began to realize that my writing was not only written "after" other works, but in *collaboration* with others and their writing, that collaboration had been the direction in which my whole set of writing activities had been moving. I am perhaps one of the most collaborative of writers in that I not only embrace other writers in my work, but include other genres, willingly mixing all sorts of forms of film, fiction, drama, art, dance, and slapstick with my poetry. And, of course, there is that aspect of collaborating with yet others — *other selves*. And, I now realize, that this is directly connected to my publishing activities as well — always a collaboration. I guess I now would describe my writing, instead of being something "after," as being work written "with."

BERNSTEIN: Well, then, perhaps you also collaborate with yourself. Can you explain how these work for you? Are they like the personae of Pessoa? If a different pseudonym was assigned to the "same" text, would it be the same work?

MESSERLI: First of all, I've always loved the idea of pseudonyms—even as a child. I still have a book that Isaac Singer signed for me in college, "to Peter Scott"—even though he knew me as his student, Douglas Messerli. He must have thought me a bit crazy! My first "real" pseudonym, however, arose out of a business necessity. Since I couldn't afford a designer for my Sun & Moon Press books, I had to design the books myself. And yet I didn't want the whole publishing enterprise to look like a one-man show. On one of the earliest books, I collaborated (there's that word again) with a local designer, Kevin Osborn. So Katie Messborn (K for Kevin, D for Douglas, Mess for Messerli, born for Osborn) sprang to life. She designed hundreds of Sun & Moon books throughout the years, and even became quite famous. I recall writer and radio personality Kenny Goldsmith wondering if he might alter a design of the one of the books for the Sun & Moon website, which I assured him would be no problem. "But I don't want to offend your wonderful designer, Katie Messborn," he replied. I assured him she wouldn't mind.

My second pseudonym arose when I was teaching literature at Temple University in Philadelphia. I was irritated in those days with the near complete abandonment by many of my colleagues of literature in favor of theory or what I would like to call "philosophical" approaches to the arts. I didn't find the theoretical writing itself to be valueless—I'd minored in philosophy and had written my PhD dissertation on narrative theory; but I did feel that using the ideas of writers such as Derrida as pedagogical "tools" in literature was a bit ridiculous. Much of it was so abstract in relation to fiction or poetry as to be nearly meaningless in a literature course. So I began to entertain one of my student-friends, Joe Ross, with the writing and sayings of my own favorite theorist, Claude Ricochet. Of course, with such a ridiculous name, it became immediately clear that Claude himself had adopted a pseudonym—his real name was Daniel Mayenne (can you believe I just had to look this up?). I had already published a manifesto under his name in a special issue I edited for *The Washington Review* on manifestos a couple of years earlier. You were in that issue, if you recall?

BERNSTEIN: Ah, yes, I remember it well. Claude and I became such close friends!

MESSERLI: And with Joe's encouragement (we both thought it all quite silly), I began to create more and more of his theory, and, since I was then working on my own theoretical work—an investigation into evil—titled *The Structure of Destruction*, I began to import some of Ricochet's statements into the three volumes. Indeed, I eventually claimed that the first two volumes were recreations of lost works (never before translated) by the author, works that I had encountered when young, one a film, the other the "incredible philosophical-historical murder mystery," *The Cross of Madame Robert*. These, moreover, were multi-genre works, allowing me to present Ricochet in all sorts of different contexts.

There is something oddly convincing about this figure. I recall when I gave poet Dennis Phillips a copy of the second volume, *The Walls Come True*, to read—it's a long performative work made up of prose poetry, drama, film, vaudeville routines, and other forms, ending with a longish Afternote about the "source"—he suggested that there were other ways in which I might handle the information about such material, in a footnote, for example. Of course, the whole Afterword was a creation/recreation of the story I'd just told in disjunctive pieces; like Faulkner's chronology of characters at the end of *The Sound and the Fury*, it is an integral part of the work.

When I was about to publish the first volume, *Along Without*, I asked Marjorie Perloff to write a blurb for the back cover copy. This work, one of the strangest I have even written, is a hybrid of film, fiction and poetry which I described in the Introduction as having been an attempt to recreate a film I saw as a young man in Norway by Claude Ricochet. Marjorie sent me a very nice blurb, supporting the existence of the French theorist and his film. I had to remind her that Ricochet was a pseudonym. Abashed, she quickly rewrote the blurb.

The National Endowment for the Arts took an early selection from the third volume, *Letters from Hanusse*, out of the fiction category for which I had submitted it, and put it into prose writing — on the basis, I suppose, of my quotes from Ricochet and, one might guess, the epistolary tone of the work as a whole.

These "readings" of the books intrigue me. For, despite the fact that I made no attempt to write at all realistically, the fact that I had used certain unexpected genres — an Introduction, an Afterword, a text peppered with seemingly academic quotes — made my character become real. The word had become flesh, so to speak. Perhaps that's why I killed him off; as the biography reports, born in 1947 — the year in which I was born — Ricochet died of AIDS in 1984 (which, had I not met my companion Howard Fox in 1970, might have been my own fate). During his short life, however, Ricochet wrote a great deal, and I have been working, and shall continue to work, to bring those pieces, in one form or another, to life. So in this one instance, my pseudonym is very close to a Pessoa heteronym, a figure locked within the author, but who exists, metaphorically speaking, in his own space. My favorite incident confirming Ricochet's existence is the time I was greeted at the Providence, Rhode Island, airport by poet Forrest Gander (whom I had not previously met) with a large sign reading CLAUDE RICOCHET.

My dramatic pseudonym, Kier Peters, is not at all like Claude. I once wrote on the back cover of one of his books that he was born in Germany, but I now doubt it, and certainly I know nothing else about him — except that "he" is the name I use to write my dramatic works. Peters came into being when I returned to drama (I wrote plays as a child). I didn't want to have to carry with me the luggage of being a so-called "experimental" poet connected with "Language" writing. I needed to (re)discover the craft and wanted to be able to imitate, in part, the plays of Albee, Pinter, Ionesco and others in order to find what worked best. Douglas Messerli, I was afraid, wouldn't be able to accomplish that; he'd have to write a much more disjunctive play if, I/he was being true to my/him self. Today I completely reject that idea — since I write so many different things. But then I needed to work outside, so to speak, of my skin. So Peters freed me to write plays that Messerli might not have wanted to.

That too is how Per Bregne was born, his name being Peter Fern in English. I've always loved the name Peter (it turns out it was my great-grandfather's name; and it's also the name of one of my nephews). My grandmother's maiden name (on my mother's side) was Fahrni (meaning Fern), and her father, back in Switzerland, was a close friend of Peter Messerli. When in a Copenhagen bookstore I decided to create Green Integer books, I thought it best to keep this new publishing activity—particularly given the numerous commitments of Sun & Moon Press—away from Douglas Messerli. Per Bregne was named as editor. And I've kept him on since, even though I've (Douglas) obviously taken on a more active role in the press.

Joshua Haigh came into being because I wanted to use a sort of 19th century trope of a manuscript delivered to my door, and to distance the difficult subjects of *Letters from Hanusse* from myself. Joshua and I, moreover, shared one close tie: we were both great admirers of Claude Ricochet. Haigh, incidentally, was my grandmother's (on my father's side) maiden name, Joshua the name of a bartender at the Cedar Bar in New York, where I wrote some of the final pages of the book.

There are others. I've actually forgotten some of them. But by and large, they're just stand-ins, beings behind whom I write. In the end, I think pseudonyms are extremely useful, almost necessary. First of all, I believe we are all many people, with many different voices possible—if we are open to them. Instead of a concept of a unified being, I much prefer a kind of Babel of existence, a body made up of all sorts of different folk speaking even sometimes contradictory statements. How much richer is this existence to the one-voice mentality! Writers, confuse yourself!, I want to shout. Make life difficult! I have always had a way of doing that.

BERNSTEIN: One way you do this, as you mentioned, is through the use of multiple genres. Indeed, much of your work is written as poetry, but also as scripts (for film, theater, and opera), and also as essays. What are the qualities of each of those genres that are of particular interest to you? How does the work of each of the genres connect?

MESSERLI: I'll start with the last part of your question: there are no differences in the sense that they constitute one activity—writing or making art. And that is what I do in nearly all my life, including publishing.

I don't know when my fascination with various genres began; I'm sure it started before reading Northrup Frye's *Anatomy of Criticism*. For I have, as long as I remember, been fascinated with genre, not just the larger genres of fiction, poetry, essay, drama, etc., but with genres within each category; my PhD dissertation focused on genres of fiction, for example, such as the anatomy, the picaresque, encyclopedic fictions, epistolary fictions, fantasy and others—I am least interested in the psychologically based, character driven genre of the novel or "roman."

Almost as soon as I started writing poetry, it became apparent that I would have to mix genres, to put narrative together with poetry and poetry with film, to imbed film within a letter. I wrote a book of poetry as a "manifesto," and in another book alternated "maxims" with "hymns." It is no accident that I claim Gertrude Stein to be my mentor, for she is a writer who single-handedly attempted nearly every literary genre, from drama, and essay, to the picaresque (*The Making of Americans*), a pastoral fiction *(Lucy Church Amiably)*, dialogue fiction (*Brewsie and Willie*), alphabetical fictions *(To Do)*, fictions based on birthdays *(Alphabets and Birthdays)*, autobiography, narrative poetry, metaphysical poetry, and numerous others—as well as psychologically driven short tales in the Flaubertian manner *(Three*

Lives). She tried everything. If one ever wanted to have a clearer understanding of genre, he should just read the total output of Stein—something very few readers have accomplished. It's an amazing outpouring of voices. A model for my own work.

In the beginning, however, I didn't know that. I just did what came naturally. Every time I had tried something and felt I succeeded, I wanted to move away from that and try something else. You know, that makes it very difficult for a writer. Readers tend to concentrate: they read *only* fiction or *only* poetry, etc. So one who writes as I do, or as Stein does, is always disappointing or at least confusing a portion of one's possible audience. Even my dearest friends have said, "Well, I like your poetry, but why do you write fiction?" or "Hey, those are great plays, but I just don't get poetry." That's a problem I've never comprehended. I guess I'm just an artistic whore, but I've always loved all the arts: visual art, dance, music, drama—all kinds of writing. You know I studied dance for a while at the Joffrey Ballet Company; I was offered a small college scholarship for voice. If I could still dance and sing, I would! In fact, I've just written a musical! At least, Kier Peters has.

BERNSTEIN: Speaking of the musical, why is *sound* so important to your poetry (at the risk of asking the most elemental poetry question of all)? Are there musical or metrical or other structures that underlie the sound patterning of your work? I wonder if you can address this, because it is to some degree a subliminal dimension, but are there particular sound patterns that you are especially drawn to, that you keep coming back to?

MESSERLI: Those are very difficult—if important— questions, and I'm not sure that I can completely answer them. You are correct, despite all the issues of genre and form that characterize my writing, it *is* sound that dominates. I suppose it began, in part, with my early musical training. Although I was not a very outstanding baritone saxophonist nor a great tenor, both activities—singing and playing in the school bands—were extremely important to me. And then, there was my great love of the Broadway musical: I would purchase original Broadway cast recordings, despite the fact that we had no record player at home! I just assimilated the importance of music and rhythm in writing. This may sound very strange to some readers, but I don't think I've ever written a sentence that doesn't have something to do with sound and rhythm—at least to my ear. Although I am always concerned with meaning, I have to admit I'd give it up in a minute if something *sounded* right.

It is not, however, just something I do in writing; I try to accomplish that "sounding," that musicality, in my everyday speech — which is probably why some people find me entertaining and others (most I admit) perceive me as a bit daff. I remember when I was teaching at Temple University, a fellow professor stopping me in the hall to give me a piece of advice: "You know, your essays sound just as if you're speaking," he observed. "Yes?" I queried. "Well, essays shouldn't sound like that. Perhaps you should read *The Yale Review*, that's what I do." I was so stunned that I must have just stammered, but I attempted to say, "Yes, you've got it. That *is* what I try to do in my essays: create a voice."

You see the problem is that what I hear as music, others don't. Many people simply can't or won't hear the rhythms and music of the voice. I just realized as I was writing this, that my closest friends — you included — all have marvelously original and musical voices. I can hear you speak, even if I haven't seen you for months!

Of course, one has to be careful in saying this, because (again we have different ears) what most people mean by voice is what they would describe as a sort of "every day, everyman" voice: the rhythms of "ordinary speech"—whatever that might mean. And that concept has allowed for the adulation of the very worst of American poetry. No, I'm talking about voices that incorporate all the richness and denseness of language, that create a kind of complex syntax that can be expressed in no other manner. No voices of *The Yale Review* or even a New England hired hand in my ears! One day, for instance, I just said out loud (to myself) "the thicket's in the thick of what / the civet cat & krait snake have / in common," and a whole poem "Scared Cows," rolled out before me. In many of my poems (those not generated by the words of other poets), I just hear a sentence in my head, a rhythm, a rhyme that I have to resist or to pun against, and that ringing brings yet another thing to mind, and another, and so on.

I'm sure there are particular sound patterns that dominate my work. When composing the opera based on my play, "Past Present Future Tense," Michael Kowalski charted out three basic syntactical and rhythmic patterns that I had used throughout. One form (again you might describe it as a kind of mini-genre) I'm very attracted to is the sort of solemn, singsong sound of old wives' tales or maxims—anything that purports to be filled with wisdom while actually revealing nonsense: "An apple, a day." I share that with Stein, whose American English is always on target: "A war is a thing where there is a man and a house and practices and was always on target." All of those marvelous unconnected conjunctions that, alas, do connect up to become the target of any war in the end. I remember reading of the great soprano Eleanor Steber's attempt to explain to a German friend the lyrics of Samuel Barber's "Summer of 1915," based on the preface to James Agee's *A Death in the Family*. "We all lie there, my mother, my father, my uncle, my aunt, and I too am lying there…." Her German friend, understandably, found the English to be absolutely ridiculous—all of those uselessly repeated pronouns. Robert Frost without a net! In English—to my ear at least—it sounds delicious!

BERNSTEIN: Do you write poetry with any pre-conceived sense of an audience, an ideal reader, or specific readers in mind?

MESSERLI: Yes, I do—me! Or Per Bregne at least. I personally have to like a poem and come to at least a temporary understanding of it, or I'll just throw it away, which I often do. In having myself for an audience, moreover, I have become very interested in the reader, any reader. I often find myself working against the reader, playing with the reader's expectations, moving the poem in one direction, but allowing it to go in another. I like the surprise of that shift and the complexity it creates—and, of course, I hope my (other) readers enjoy it as well.

More recently, however, I've become a bit less conscious of an audience—including me as the audience. The newer work, since it comes from a kind of emotional abstraction, doesn't really depend as much on the audience or the reader for me. I mean, *I want readers*. I guess, I'm just less worried about them. Perhaps it's because one finally recognizes that there are so few! When poets begin to worry about their readers—and it happens every day—I get nervous: either they have nothing else to say or they have been writing poetry for all the wrong reasons. I feel that I *have* to write. I have no choice in the matter. So, in that sense, well who gives a damn if I have legions of loyal admirers? Or that everyone understands what I have been trying to express? It's not that I don't seek out a response, but if that is really what one's after, one should immediately stop writing and find an easier way of expression.

BERNSTEIN: Through Sun & Moon Press and now Green Integer, you have been one of the most, possibly *the* most active publishers of literary translations in the United States? At a time when most other American publishers are backing away from literary translations (and translations of poetry, of which you do many, are the most rare item of all), can you discuss the motivations for this aspect of your publishing and editing and also your overall plans in this area, including the PIP series?

MESSERLI: Oh my, that sounds so apocalyptic! I hope it's not just up to me! But yes, I probably do publish more translation—particularly poetry—than any other American publisher. I have come to have an absolute passion for it—publishing international writing. In a time when we Americans seem to be further insulating ourselves from the rest of the world (perhaps one should say "alienating" ourselves), it just seems more and more important that we share the languages, ideas, and emotions of people from other cultures and countries. I have to admit that when I began publishing—although I have always loved international writing and read a good deal of it—I was pretty smug about American poetry and fiction. I thought it was some of the very best writing that had ever been done. I don't recall when things began to change—it happened long before Jerome Rothenberg's and Pierre Joris's voluminous double-volume anthology of world poetry, *Poems for the Millennium*—but I began to discover that there were not just a few great writers from nearly every country, but dozens of important figures. Turkey, for example, did not just have the two poets represented by the Rothenberg-Joris anthology (Nazim Hikmet and Ece Ayhan), but a number of truly innovative poets, including Oktay Rifat, Orhan Veli, Ilhan Berk, Edip Cansever, Cemal Sureya, and Melih Cevdet Anday. Luigi Ballerini and Paul Vangelisti introduced me to a large group of brilliant Italian poets, an anthology of which I published for Sun & Moon Press. My friend Peter Glassgold showed me through his *Living Space* anthology that 20th century Dutch poetry had been stunningly originally through the works of Lucebert, Bert Shierbeek, Jan Elburg, Gerrit Kouwenaar, Remco Campert, Hugo Claus and others. People like Régis Bonvicino (along with Elizabeth Bishop's early Brazilian anthology) showed me the writings of outstanding Brazilians such as João Cabral de Melo Neto, Murilo Mendes, Carlos Drummond de Andrade, José Oswald de Souza Andrade, and Raul Bopp—to name just a few. The more I read, the more I discovered, until I realized that almost every country had had exciting poets throughout the century, poets just as adventurous, often *more* adventurous than Pound, Williams, or Stevens. I'm still in awe, years later. Americans need to discover that, far from being at the center of things, they are just as often at the fringes; instead of their self-proclaimed role as leaders, they are just as often followers—at least in literature; and I suspect if I were to investigate other fields of knowledge that I'd discover that we Americans often live in a vacuum when it comes to knowing what else exists.

You know, it's interesting, having this knowledge about world poetry doesn't simply make me feel a bit humbled and embarrassed for my own countrymen's limitations. It has helped me to be a richer and more complex American writer—and I think it would help all American poets. It was that which Pound was trying to explain to Williams, get to know the world! Williams mistakenly thought Pound was asking him to write like the Europeans (or perhaps Asians). As great a poet as he is—and I do think Williams is a great poet—imagine what he might have written had he been able to read the works of Huidobro or Girondo or Xul Solar, Andrade! Would he still have written *Asphodel, That Greeny Flower*?

I'm truly intoxicated with all the variety of poetry I've discovered. I know this can sound a bit like worst kind of American tourist, someone bitten by the exotic, fascinated with the difference of things. But I truly don't think that that's the issue. More often, in fact, one can see grand similarities, different cultures, each in their own, coming to perceptions at the very same moment, or discover important connections, influences.

I'm so lucky, I think, to be able to help American readers discover this work. It would be wonderful to think it might somehow even change us, but that's the missionary in me. Even if we just accept it at its surface value, and take in the pleasure of reading these poets, what a wonderful task I've set for myself.

As I said previously, however, I have ways of making things difficult, and my grand plans for the publication of this work is more than a bit insane. I plan for at least 50 volumes of the *PIP Anthology of International Poetry of the 20th Century* — and we're just on volume 5. I've also just begun a fiction series, *1001 Great Stories*, of which I hope to publish two volumes of 10 stories each in every season. You understand that, given my current age, I would have to live to at least 82 to accomplish this? I'll do what I can.

BERNSTEIN: How did you come to publish *Nothing the Sun Could Not Explain* — the important anthology of Brazilian poetry, edited by Régis Bonvicino and Nelson Ascher? What was the reception of the book?

MESSERLI: Actually, I don't completely recall. I don't know if then San Francisco counsel João Almino first contacted me, or Michael Palmer, who was working with João to see this book published in English. But one or the other sent me the manuscript, and, since I had just finished my own huge American anthology, and was planning the Italian one, I immediately accepted it. It was published by Sun & Moon Press in 1997, and it quite quickly sold out of its first printing. It wasn't until I traveled to Brazil, however, that I came to really understand just how important such an anthology of younger poets can be. This was the first anthology of its kind since Elizabeth Bishop's *An Anthology of Twentieth-Century Brazilian Poetry* of 1972, and accordingly, it was enormously important in Brazil. Suddenly, I wished I'd been more active in the actual editing of it. Michael and Régis, the primary editors, had done a splendid job. But I quickly realized that we could have used more information on each poet and a more careful editorial eye. So instead of rushing to reprint it on Sun & Moon Press—which was having its financial problems—I worked with Régis over a couple of years to bring it into the format of the PIP series, which included more extensive biographies, complete listings of the authors' books, and a more careful presentation of the poems; we also added one poet, deleting another. I'm very proud of the new edition.

BERNSTEIN: Would you speak of your own relation to Brazilian poetry? Have you any particular affinity for, or difficulty with, Portuguese, a language that for many Americans is the least familiar of the colonial languages of the Americas (English, French, Spanish, Portuguese)?

MESSERLI: I think I've already made it clear that my ability with languages other than English is limited. I would have to live in Brazil for several months before the language might reach my brain. I do not find it impossible to read articles in the newspapers, particularly if I have the context, since Spanish does help. Hearing it, on the other hand—although it's a wonderful sounding language—it's impossible for me to understand. The Brazilians also make it quite clear that they do not speak the Portuguese of Portugal. So...what can I say? What I know of Brazilian literature is from translation.

In truth, although I love many of the great 20th century Brazilian writers and many of younger poets we published in *Nothing the Sun Could Not Explain* I've not really been influenced (yet) by the poetry. Certainly São Paulo, the city, got into my blood, particularly on my second visit. What an incredible place! And I wrote a play in São Paulo (having witnessed one of my own plays performed there). So perhaps Kier Peters was influenced. I think a third visit will be necessary.... And I haven't even seen Rio! The important thing, however, is that I truly feel I have friends there, particularly in Régis, Horácio Costa (who took me on marvelous tours of the city where some are afraid to go), and Claudia Roquette-Pinto.

BERNSTEIN: Now to broaden the question just a bit, have the poetries and poetics of the Americas—Brazil, South and Central America, the Caribbean—been a significant frame of reference to you? In what way does this figure differently for you than your connection to European poetries?

MESSERLI: That's a very interesting question that I haven't really thought carefully enough about. I'd begin by saying that there are figures, important figures, Neruda, Huidobro, Girondo, Bopp, Asturias, Cortázar, Donoso, Bioy-Casares, Borges, and Fuentes, who have meant a great deal to me. But I don't know if their being South or Central Americans or Mexicans makes that influence different from the European—or Middle Eastern or Asian influences I've felt. I guess, in part, it's simply because I've traveled less in South and Central America than in Europe. You know, I've only been to Brazil—not even to Mexico!! In that sense, I'm as isolated as I've described most Americans. I haven't yet assimilated or, perhaps we should say, even experienced what the Caribbean or South or Central America is all about. I will say that of the region of which you're speaking, I find the Cuban authors—authors that, coincidentally, are also mostly gay—Sarduy, Lezama Lima, Cabrera Infante, Piñera most *simpatico*. But then, I've never been to Cuba either. The literature of the Caribbean, Central and South America, however, moves me, and leads me into desiring a closer relationship, a deeper comprehension.

BERNSTEIN: At the time I am writing this question, the U.S. is struggling through a most important Presidential election (and by the time this is published, the results of that election will be known). Speaking specifically from your perspective as a poet, how do you view the current political climate in the U.S.? How does the work of poetry affect the political sphere?

MESSERLI: I've already expressed some of my fears in a previous conversation with Régis Bonvicino in the pages of this journal. Along with many of my friends, I am, quite frankly terrified by the current political climate, and am afraid of what might happen if President Bush is reelected. I believe—even if it's just symbolic—we have lost a great many of our personal freedoms since 9/11 and the war in Iraq. And I don't foresee that some of these freedoms—including our ability to travel to certain countries like Cuba—is going to improve. I just published a translation of a wonderful Cuban poet, Reina María Rodríguez; however The Patriot Act seems to suggest that, as a publisher, I might be subject to a fine or imprisonment for having "improved" (which the government appears to consider "translation" as accomplishing) her writing. I can't believe that our government would be so insane as to actually act on such a provision, but...there it is. This is a real fear which we all must face. I think it has had a terribly stultifying effect on American poetry and the arts in general. In today's *Los Angeles Times*, for example, there was a congratulatory piece on how wonderfully the current head of the National Endowment for the Arts, Dana Gioia, was getting along with the conservatives in Congress. Meanwhile, he has created two new programs at the National Endowment, one to bring Shakespearian productions to American communities, and the other, titled "Operation Homecoming," to bring poets and novelists to military installations to conduct writing workshops for veterans of Iraq and Afghanistan. I have severe doubts about the artistic integrity of both of these programs; but, more important, he has set a dangerous precedent in defining what artistic projects should be supported by the government. While other projects, less specifically aimed at one constituency, are certain to be supported by the NEA, I see this as a terribly frightening development. Upon being sworn into his position, Gioia was asked if he had any specific agenda: he answered, "I'm a Republican but I'm not political." It's hard to imagine how to say anything profound in the context of such doublespeak. And then, there's the country at large, the American press...

BERNSTEIN: Exactly a decade ago, you edited and published the most comprehensive collection of innovative and exploratory American poetry of the period, *From the Other Side of the Century: A New American Poetry 1960–1990*. If you were to extend that anthology forward to the next decade, to the present, what would be the most significant changes and additions you would make—not only in terms of the names of poets you might add or subtract, but of new directions and how they may now affect your view of the entire period after 1960?

MESSERLI: Has it really been a decade? Yes, I guess it has. We are definitely now on "the other side of the century."

In part, I am having to consider some of those choices, since I am now republishing that volume (1,135 pages in its original form), in four PIP anthology volumes, each with a new introduction. But since I do not want to have to repurchase the rights, which if I substantially changed it, making it another edition, I'd have to do, I am leaving it basically intact. Since its original publication, moreover, the book has become something of an icon, a beloved statement in its own right—on the internet it's even been proclaimed as one of the "best books of the century!" So, I want to leave it as its own statement in time and place.

Looking at it as objectively as I can, moreover, I wouldn't suggest that there are any new major developments. A few younger figures certainly might be added to one section or another, but I don't have the feeling that a new "grouping" or poetic expression has yet developed. Perhaps it is just the time in which we live, but—while younger poets have demonstrated interest in their own generation—no ideological force has seemed to bring them together, to help them to cohere. There's certainly a lot of poetic writing today in the U.S.—and some of it quite competent—but I can't yet perceive it as coming out of any generational need or desire. I do see a few poets moving toward what I might describe as a poetry imbedded with the language and ideas of technology and other scientific terminology, which is somewhat interesting. And, occasionally, as in the work of Joe Ross or Mark Wallace, I see increasingly a political subtext. But overall, much of the writing is lyrically quite stunning, but basically centered upon self and perception—concerns that might be equally at home in the New York School.

In short, I don't see the need yet to alter or revise my anthology. But I hope I'm wrong, and that someone will edit a new anthology of younger writers that will show me what I was missing. Isn't that why new anthologies are published?

BERNSTEIN: Finally, one of your largest-scale projects at the moment is called "Being American." Please talk about this work.

MESSERLI: Actually, it's escalated into two volumes, "Being American" and "Being UnAmerican," so it's rather appropriate for this discussion.

For years friends (even enemies for that matter) have tried to get me to write a memoir. I certainly have known a lot of literary and other major figures of our time, and I guess they think I have something say about them and need to explain what I have been up to. But you know, I just am not the type of person who is comfortable with writing a memoir centered, as memoirs are, on the self. As I said early in this interview, I'm a collaborator.

Also, I think you have to have a sense of a somewhat coherent life to want to sit down and write about it. I have had no such experience. I've lived in dozens of different houses in numerous towns in the US and overseas. The longest period in one place has been my last 18 years here in Los Angeles. My life, accordingly, is broken up into episodes, bits and pieces, with large gaping holes where I can't remember events or individuals.

What I *have* done over the years is to write a great deal about other writers, artists, dancers, musicians, etc. Moreover, as I expressed it earlier, my life is, in a sense, *art*—at least I understand my life through art. So I began to gather some of these essays and reviews written long ago, clearing them of cobwebs—academicism (when I could) and my own failure to carefully edit. I have also worked to make these pieces more personal, as if there were an actual voice speaking behind them. To these, I have added shorter pieces, sort of an ongoing commentary about my experience with different films, poems, fiction, dances, works of art, etc: Why, when I was 12 years old, did I so thoroughly enjoy Hitchcock's *Vertigo*, for example, and yet at 13, hate *North by Northwest*—a movie I now love? Why is it that no one talks about the obvious (to me at least) gay subtext of Cary Grant's *Bringing Up Baby*? Why

I feel that, far from being, as many see it, a paean to American innocence, the musical *Oklahoma!* is filled with the violence and disregard for justice that characterizes much of contemporary American life. I just wrote an essay, for example, on "Three Children of the Fifties: Holden, Lolita, Malcolm." I have also included other information, my personal memories of some of the figures I'm writing about, etc. So it *has* become a kind of memoir, one centered on my cultural experiences as opposed to events in my life.

Of course, as I've established, I also have done just as much writing and thinking about other cultures, about the art of other countries. So I had to create the second volume, "Being UnAmerican," to talk about the other half of my cultural life. I guess if I include this interview, it would appear in the second volume.

In any event, I'm thoroughly enjoying this, which I imagine should take a number of years — making it, ultimately, too ungainly and voluminous to ever be published. I repeat: I have a way of making things difficult.

September 7–12, 2004

Reprinted from *Jacket*, no. 28 (October 2005)

Two Works by Julien Gracq

THE INTRUSION

JULIEN GRACQ **AU CHÂTEAU D'ARGOL** (PARIS: JOSÉ CORTI, 1938), TRANSLATED FROM THE FRENCH BY LOUISE VARÈSE AS **THE CASTLE OF ARGOL** (NORFOLK, CONNECTICUT: J. LAUGHLIN, 1951); REPRINTED BY (VENICE, CALIFORNIA: THE LAPIS PRESS, 1991)

CIRCLING FORWARD

JULIEN GRACQ **LA PRESQU'ILE** [LA ROUTE/LA ROI COPHETUA] (PARIS: JOSÉ CORTI, 1970)
UNPUBLISHED TRANSLATION OF **LA PRESQU'ILE** AS **THE PENINSULA** BY ELIZABETH DESHAYS, SENT TO ME IN JULY 2005

Julien Gracq

Each September or October since 1994 several literary friends and I have chosen a writer who we felt made a major contribution throughout his or her lifetime to literature. There is, alas, no money involved with this "award,"; we see The America Awards, despite the name, less as an award than as a recognition. Given the annual mediocrity of choices by the Booker Prize, Pulitzer Prize, American Book Awards, and, often, the Nobel Literature Prize committees , we felt—in the manner of World Literature Today's Neustadt International Prize, that we could bring attention to deserving figures in literature without all the back-room political and social commitments of those prizes. I have been quite proud of our choices: beginning with the Martinique poet Aimé Cesaire in 1994, we have chosen some rather remarkable women and men, including a couple, José Donoso and Rafael Alberti, just a few weeks before their deaths. Only once have we chosen a figure awarded a Nobel Prize, José Saramago in 2004, but this year (2005) the Nobel literature committee chose one of the authors who we had previously honored, Harold Pinter (our recognition came in 1995). For 2006, we chose to recognize the noted French novelist Julien Gracq. Below is my tribute to him in the form a brief commentary on two of his books.

The Intrusion

Described by its author as a fiction using obvious literary references (Wagner, Nietzsche, Poe and others) around the belief that the redeemer-savior is often also the destroyer, Gracq's *The Castle of Argol* is, on another level, a highly romantic homoerotic tale. A young man of great wealth and intelligence, Albert, purchases a castle and the surrounding landscape. He moves into Argol and immediately perceives the mystery and magic of its surroundings, particularly the nearby forest of Storrvan, a threatening overgrowth of towering trees. Suddenly he receives a message that his dear friend and soul-mate Herminien is planning a visit — along with a stranger named Heide. Herminien and Albert, who have roomed together as students, see themselves as almost twins, each able to intellectually stimulate each other beyond the range of all others, and each able to read one another's deepest thoughts. As Albert prepares for their arrival, he visits the nearby desolate seashore, discovering there a graveyard. On the surface of one tombstone he inscribes the name of the strange visitor: Heide. Clearly, Heide is already an intruder; but upon her arrival he is mesmerized by her beauty and intelligence. Over the next months, a deep relationship develops between the two, galling

Herminien and inspiring his festering hatred. He recognizes that he has brought Heide to Albert for his friend's tacit approval and to enable him to share his love for Heide. But Albert also seems strangely aloof and cold with regard to Heide's sexuality.

One afternoon Heide and Herminien sneak away into the forest, failing to return by sunset. Intrigued and almost hypnotized by their disappearance and the forest itself, Albert follows them into the dark woods, only to discover the body of Heide, brutally raped by his friend. He takes her to the castle and nurses her back to health. A long time later, they both follow a cleared path through the forest and discover the body of Herminien, who has been thrown by his horse. He too is returned to the castle and restored, but a new hatred develops in Albert regarding him. Heide remains secluded in her room, obviously unable to face either of them, while Herminien and Albert return to their conversations. Heide commits suicide, and they bury her in the seaside graveyard. Herminien determines to leave, but Albert follows him into the wood, putting a dagger into his side. A brilliantly abstract and hallucinatory tale.

Los Angeles, July 12, 2005

Circling Forward

Julien Gracq's short fiction, *La Presqu'ile (The Peninsula)* (1970) is a deceptively simple work with regard to plot. Simon waits at the Brévenay train station in Brittany for Irmgard, although she has warned him that her arrival at midday is "very unlikely." The woman, with whom he has obviously had previous sexual rendevouses, does not arrive, and he has little to do but await the evening train. A methodical man, he determines to spend the afternoon driving along the Brittany coast and arranging for their eventual journey. He returns that evening to the train station to meet her.

Little else "happens"—if one defines plot as Americans might. But in Gracq's beautifully lyrical tale, *everything* happens on the emotional level as the reader participates in Simon's embracement of the flora and fauna, the light, the sounds, and smells of Brittany, where he has evidently spent his childhood. Traveling through small towns along the coast, Simon encounters the sensations of his past, alternatively overcome with highly pitched pleasure and disgust tinged with a feeling of emptiness. Indeed, the whole fiction may be perceived in the context of Simon's alternating emotional responses as he drives through the landscape, stopping at various locations, sometimes just to take in the natural scene or to observe the view.

It soon becomes clear that Simon is not only methodical, but experiences life most fully at a slight remove from it. It is vistas of the ocean, not direct contact with it, that he finds most pleasurable. His favorite time of the day is the moment when it begins to fade in late afternoon, with workers returning home, light pouring from windows. As he moves across a Brittany peppered with recognizable small towns and locations that Gracq has renamed to create a mythological quality, we also begin to connect the various allusions to Tristan and Isolde with the relationship between Simon and Irmgard. It becomes clear that the rising and falling patterns of Simon's emotional state resemble the endless waves of passion and hate that define the famous legend, which in the original version took place in Brittany. Indeed, Simon alternates in his feelings for Irmgard as well, sometimes imagining her every movement with sexual anticipation, at other times forgetting what she looks like, dreading their encounter.

As the day moves forward into night, the anticipation heightens as the reader can only wonder — as he stops in the small town of Coatliguen, briefly pauses on the isle of Eprun, and listens near an isolated country home to the removed sounds of a mother and daughter speaking within — whether or not Simon will reach the station in time. For Simon, it is clear, is a conflicted soul, a figure of great sensitivity and desire, but also a person who prefers his distance from others, who cannot make lasting commitments. As he arrives at the station and watches the train enter the yard, he stands at the other side of the crossing, a barrier of metal bars before him, wondering "How can I get to her?" The potentiality remains, but, one suspects, their love may remain unfulfilled.

Los Angeles, July 8, 2005

Standstill

HANS FAVEREY, **AGAINST THE FORGETTING:
SELECTED POEMS,** TRANSLATED BY FRANCIS R. JONES
(NEW YORK: NEW DIRECTIONS, 2004)

Hans Faverey

Born in 1933 in Paramaribo, Surinam, poet Hans Faverey moved to Amsterdam as a child and lived there until his death in 1990. Faverey was one of those rare individuals who combined the scientific mind—he worked as a clinical psychologist—with music—he played and composed for the harpsichord—and poetry—he published eight volumes of poems and won several of major Dutch literary awards.

Now, through the good graces of New Directions and translator Francis R. Jones we have a new US edition of his selected poems, *Against the Forgetting*. Faverey wrote short abstractly modulated lyrics, most often in sequences or cycles. Unfortunately, in this collection we get very few complete sequences, with 28 of the 33 sequences represented being incomplete. It is difficult therefore to get the sense of Faverey's poetic "pace" in English. It appears the separate sections of each sequence are only tangentially related with regard to images and subject matter, and are generally connected only through formal devices; but it would have helped to have a just a few more complete cycles in translation to see how they function.

One of my favorite works of the volume presents a complete cycle: "Chrysanthemums, Rowers," which begins with a seemingly static image: chrysanthemums in a vase on a table, an image Faverey immediately deflates as, with Gertrude Stein-like logic, he reverses himself: "these / are not the chrysanthemums / which are by the window / on the table / in the vase." Clearly, the words with which he has begun are meant to be understood differently from a still-life in someone's house or apartment. As he makes clear in the second part of the cycle, these words are like a photograph, an image of something real, a mirror of reality which, like a mirror, reverses its image (just as he has reversed his original image in the second stanza of the poem), making it difficult for the perceiver to recognize that it represents himself and the world in which he stands. As objects, moreover, photograph and mirror cannot recognize anyone. It is only in the human mind, one's own living hand or "a hand that wants to belong to me" that actually "is" something that, as it covers the eyes, can be understand as a part of the self coming towards one from space. Objects, like the still-life he has first presented, might be misunderstood as revealing meaning, but it is only as these objects are internalized in thought that their "meaning" can be revealed. The poet perceives "The utter emptiness / in every thing, which actually is." Mind over matter, so to speak, is Favery's true subject in this poem; as the rowers row further inland, in their mythology, they row until the water is gone, rowing into the overgrown landscape, a land without rowers, an "over- / rown land." The final pun closes the argument, as we recognize the poem as a thing of art, an artifice as opposed to mimesis or a representation.

Even though the translator does not feature many such complete texts, the reader does quickly perceive that this issue is at the heart of most of Favery's writing, and the processes of composing and decomposing, building and unbuilding a world of language, are at the heart of his vision. I will present three examples as a kind of random evidence of this pattern in Favery's poems:

It is snowing

but is no longer snowing.
When it started to snow
I went to the window;

I went missing.

Sometime then,

just before the snow started
falling again, into great,

ever slower flakes,
it must also have

stopped snowing.

[from "Sur place"]

*

Now it is here;

now it is not-here.
How it thrusts through itself
takes place between not yet

and nevermore. Once under

way, it moves neither where
it is, nor where it is not.
Given free rein
it keeps slipping from who
stands fast: now from one

now from another....

[from "My Little Finger"]

*

Where the apricot tree
stood still then
I stand still now.

Between the gladioli
I know the spot
where she stood then:
she threw me the apricot—
then. Now,

as memory does with itself
what it will, we begin
biting once more, almost
in unison, between

the maize plants; she her
apricot, I my apricot;

while the little foxes still prowl
through the vineyard, and the sea,
whispering: she is not with me;
no, you will not find it here;
she is not in me.

[from "Lightfall"]

In the earliest poems of this collection, this process of evolving and devolving images and language results in a kind of "standstill," a word repeated in several of Faverey's poems. The poet alternates between these two actions as he moves from the "real" world (or perhaps we should say the "unreal" world) of space to the world of the mind, the truly "real" world of experience. As each "reality" takes back its own meaning, the reader is left with a sense of emptiness—like a lover who was there but is no longer, like a perceiver who, in lifting a stone, finds in his hand an object that is "no longer a stone," but a thing of language.

In later work Faverey recasts this image of a "standstill" into a image of a spider at work on its web, a Penelope-like figure who weaves and unweaves each day, destroying its creation and itself in the very process of creating it:

> The dolphin swimming in front of the ship
> keeps swimming in front of the ship
> until there is definitely no longer
> a dolphin swimming in front of a ship.

Favery's work, accordingly, will not be for those who see a poem as a lifesaver of meaning in a world a chaos. Rather, his poems reveal the process of life itself as an ever-shifting, changing force that destroys the perception at the very moment of perceiving the world's "merciless beauty."

Los Angeles, September 21, 2005

Reprinted from *The Green Integer Review*, NO. 1 (January–February 2006) and *Jacket*, NO. 31 (2006)

The Hole: Missing Robert Creeley

ROBERT CREELEY, **WORDS** (NEW YORK: SCRIBNER'S, 1967).

The William Carlos Williams Centennial Conference was held at the University of Maine in Orono, August 24–26, 1983.
At this conference were numerous poets and critics, including Kenneth Burke, Robert Creeley, Allen Ginsberg, Hugh Kenner, Paul Mariani, and Diane Wakoski.

Douglas Messerli observes an altercation between a customer and a look-alike Robert Creeley in a bar in Philadelphia in late 1984.

Auckland Sunday Star

Robert Creeley

The death of Robert Creeley a few weeks ago has left me with a somewhat empty feeling, not so much because of a relationship, but because of one that had been promised—as if I had awakened from a kind of dreamscape of what might have been. Even the location of his death, Texas—whose landscape I always imagine as a vast empty space, like that depicted in the movie *Giant*—seems, to my way of thinking, slightly surreal given the fact that Creeley who seemed to be defined by the New England where he was born and spent most of his life.

It's not that I knew Creeley well. In fact, I hardly knew him, and when we were together, I was tongue-tied—a strange admission for one who seems to some friends to suffer from logorrhea. I believe we first met—although I am certain we had previous correspondence—at a 1983 conference in Orono, Maine, devoted to the poetry of William Carlos Williams. Creeley was one of several poetry-world celebrities in attendance. Allen Ginsberg and I had several conversations at the event. The elderly Kenneth Burke and I spoke about Djuna Barnes. And at the first night's lobster feast I was seated across from Hugh Kenner, who was later outraged when, during his presentation, a young friend of Ginsberg strolled naked through the lecture hall! I even had a short chat with Diane Wakoski, a poet for whom I have no great admiration.

But Bob and I, who spent part of a day together, if I remember correctly, hardly said a word; we just smiled.

Now I know the many rumors about Creeley, about his violent drinking bouts and his sometimes uncontrollable temper. Later I'd hear gossip about how difficult he'd been to his fellow colleagues at Buffalo, particularly to Charles Bernstein (although Charles, who doesn't gossip, has never said a negative word to me about their relationship). To me, he seemed always a bit shy—if extremely intense. One evening during the conference several of the poets spoke of their relationships with and to Williams. Ginsberg glibly repeated his encounters with the legend, focusing, as Allan almost always did, on his own persona. But Creeley, speaking in a hushed voice that could hardly be heard in the large lecture hall, spoke quite brilliantly about what Williams offered a young poet just coming of age in the late 1940s. Williams' best works, in my estimation, were some of his earliest: *Kora in Hell* and *Spring and All*. But Creeley made it clear that even later works of the poet had had an enormous impact on American writers of the time. I was spellbound by his insights; I even took notes (and now wish I'd saved them).

I can't recall now whether I saw Creeley again. I seem to remember a party in New York — perhaps at Charles Bernstein's place — where Creeley was in attendance. I vaguely remember being unable to communicate once more.

But I did correspond and he always answered. Our longest correspondence had to do with the selection of his poetry in my omnibus anthology, *From the Other Side of the Century: A New American Poetry 1960–1990*. After making my selections for this volume, I sent the list of chosen poems to each poet, asking for his or her reactions. Most of the poets simply accepted my list, but Creeley was slightly suspicious about my choices — several of which were not the standard anthology selections. I responded by writing a very long letter, summarizing the forms and themes of each poem I selected, and explaining why these elements of the poems had made me choose them for inclusion. I suspect those notes sit in files at the University of California-San Diego library, but I am slightly embarrassed for them, imagining now how simplistic my comments must have been. Perhaps writing, on this occasion, on one of his poems might redeem any reductive qualities of my previous comments. I do recall, moreover, some of what I wrote about "The Hole," one of my favorites, and a work highly appropriate for this short essay.

I explained to him that despite the common themes of his work—"love," "mother," "dying and aging"—that what I responded most to in his writing was the form. The words, as in "The Hole," are almost always simple, slightly aphoristic.

"There is a silence to fill," begins the poem, reminding one almost of Frost's "Something there is that doesn't love a wall." But whereas Frost's first line is just that, a wall, a long line of narrative statement, Creeley's observation is in constant action, as he breaks down its component parts: "There is," "a silence," "to fill. A." The structure of the poem itself nicely mirrors its meaning as the words tug against themselves, allowing for a kind of breakdown in communication, a stuttering of meaning which is beautifully expressed through the onomatopoetic lines following:

A
foot, a fit

fall,
filled.

Indeed, the stanza break has produced a kind of fall; the foot has tripped as the rhythm of the poem (the poetic foot) has exploded into disjunctive nouns and verbs, present and past. Creeley restates the poetic action in another aphorism, which contains the image of someone carrying a container of liquid: "If / you are / not careful all / [stanza break] the water spills." The "foot" of the previous stanza is suddenly restored as an image of someone bearing water who—if the reader is determined to fill up the scene with narrative—arriving at the hole, fits the foot into it and falls. Or nearly so.

But suddenly the poem seems to take a different direction as the narrator recounts his own actions of taking off his bathing suit in a lake and peeing into the water with pleasure. Here the emptying of liquid is repeated as he links it, through this short narrative, with the "other end," the hole—the ass wiped clean. That "hole," in turn, calls up the image of the opposite sex, through the vagina, with which the narrator associates the renowned revelation in the 1921 trial of movie comedian Fatty Arbuckle's alleged rape of Virginia Rappe with a Coke bottle, resulting in her death.*

The narrator further associates this image—the quite brutal filling of a hole—with his first sexual encounters with a woman, who, evidently, screamed in horror as he touched her, later admitting that "it felt right." Accordingly, the "hole" is associated throughout the rest of the work as both pleasurable release and sexual misconduct, as the poet/narrator further recalls an incident in which his teacher, exposing himself, released, like the narrator earlier in the poem, his urine. Accordingly, throughout the poem pleasure and pain are brought together as the hole is transformed from a location or object into a great emptiness of emotional needs waiting to be filled with language and love. At all times, moreover, the very structure of the poem, the many enjambments, breaks, and fissures of words and line and the jumps of narrative content, reflect the same mixture of emptiness and fulfillment, of terrifying space and linguistic enrichment. Within its subject matter and the multiple shifts and stutters of expression, this small poem takes on an almost operatic quality, resembling somewhat *Tristan and Isolde*'s recurring *coitus interruptus* as narrator/poem moves forward, falls, nearly spills his/its contents, only to push forward again. By the end of this work both narrator and reader have reached nearly uncontrollable desire ("I / can't wait any / longer") to fill the hole both sexually and psychically.

Even now this brief summary somewhat embarrasses me: the poem presents its ideas in its succinct language so much better! Perhaps it is this feeling of inadequacy of expressing such a dense complex of ideas in such concentrated form that accounted from my being unable to speak freely with Creeley himself. In any event, Creeley must have appreciated my attempts to explain his work to him since, with only one or two small exceptions, he agreed to my original selections and even allowed my inclusion of his work within the grouping of the so-called Language poets.

Over the years we continued occasionally to correspond. He participated in the collaborative collection of poetry, *Between*, with a rather humorous put-down of my poetic concern (taken from lines and words of his own poetry) about the "distance" between *here* and *there*. "*Here's* where / Comes *There*. [stanza break] If you do, / They will too."

Yet it seems as if, with Bob Creeley, I was always *here* while he was always *there*, and we could never quite find a ground on which to stand as the friends we recognized ourselves to be. There was a "hole," a sort of emptiness waiting to be filled, between us.

---

* The alleged rape of Virginia Rappe occurred on September 5th, 1921. Roscoe Conkling ["Fatty"] Arbuckle endured three trials, the first of which began in November 1921, resulting in a hung jury. The second trial also saw the jury deadlocked. The third trial, beginning in March 1922, acquitted him, with the jury writing a formal apology for the treatment he had received in the courts. His career, however, was destroyed.

Addendum: The Murder Of Robert Creeley

Given what I have just recounted, it seems appropriate that I tell my strange story about an encounter with Creeley that never existed.

It must have been during my last year of teaching at Temple University, 1984, about a year after the Williams conference in Maine that this event occurred. From time to time, I would drop in at a very dreary bar on Spruce Street. The bar was what most people would describe as a dive, attached — although I only realized this after — to a resident hotel, which I was later told was filled with cross-dressers and transsexuals. The bar was poorly lit, but I sensed that in the back there were one or two billiard or pool tables, around which several seedy figures hovered. I went there because they had the best (and greasiest) fried chicken and French fries in Philadelphia.

I had just ordered my dinner when I observed, sitting at another corner of the three-sided bar, a man who bore an extremely strong resemblance to Robert Creeley; he even wore a patch over one eye, which Creeley often did. With him was a young blond male, quite effeminate and clearly gay. Generally, I would have ignored them both, focusing instead on the unhealthy basket just placed before me. But

I couldn't get the image of Bob Creeley out of my head. It appeared that the young man was upset about something, and "Creeley" was trying to smooth over the situation, to calm him down a bit. It was not that the boy was actually crying, but rather that he was occasionally whimpering. Creeley seemed to me to have a calming effect with whispered phrases which I imagined to be something like "It will be okay" or "You're all right now." The blond, however, was apparently not to be reasoned with.

The incident—if you can call it that, for one might simply have conceived the interchanges as a mild lover's spat—erupted every so often as I consumed my fries and drank my beer. In a short while, moreover, it became apparent that the man sitting closest to this couple was not at all happy with what was transpiring. Suddenly, he shouted over at Creeley, "You leave Bobby alone!"

I was startled and confused by the statement. Who was Bobby? How had he come to know him, the blond kid? In my confusion of thought, the older man—the one who looked like Creeley—was Bobby! The shouter's intrusion into this situation was disturbing.

The boy continued to fidget, with the Creeley look-alike trying to comfort him. Bobby wouldn't, however, be comforted. And the man beside them spoke up once again: "I'm warning you, leave Bobby alone."

I tried to imagine what the situation must have been. Was Bobby, the boy, a local denizen of the hotel, and had the Creeley fellow and he just had sex? Were there drugs involved? Perhaps that's why the young man was so confused and dazed-looking. I couldn't help wondering what had this intruder thought Creeley had done to Bobby? Why was he warning him? It appeared to me that Creeley was already leaving Bobby alone.

But neither Bobby nor the other drinker, it appeared, were satisfied. Bobby whimpered and wrestled away from Creeley's gentle strokes. The man beside them was glowering with hate. Then everything came to a head. A knife instantly appeared in the man's fist. Creeley quietly protested. "I'm not hurting him," he insisted. "I'm not doing anything!"

I was horrified! Was I about to witness the murder of Robert Creeley? For he had actually *become* Bob Creeley in my uncomprehending head. He not only looked like Creeley, he *moved* like Creeley, he *spoke* like Creeley. To me, he was the poet himself.

I saw the bartender bend down and push some button, and then rise up with a gun in his hand! "Put the knife down," he commanded.

Suddenly, the bar door opened and what appeared to be a gang poured in. Yet this wasn't the kind of "gang" that word usually connotes. First of all, the leader was dressed all in white, perhaps — although my memory is a bit vague on this — even wearing a tie. He was incredibly handsome, a young Adonis. And the rest of gang members were equally well-dressed, all of them quite attractive. What kind of gang was this? A junior version of the noted Philadelphia mafia? A sort of neighborhood protection group? Yet this was not a gathering of the usual neighborhood do-gooders for, at that very moment, I had the impression that they were all gay!

Before I even could assimilate their presence, they scooped up Creeley and took him away, disappearing into the night with the "culprit" as quickly as they had come. And just as suddenly, the men hovering in the back of bar came forward into the light *en masse*. "Are you all right, Bobby? Is everything okay? Poor Bobby." Each of these scraggly beings had their own phrase, and each had to come forward and put their hands upon the object of their concerns and love. I could make no sense of anything unfolding in front of me now. I quietly put down some money and escaped.

I was never to see Robert Creeley — nor his look-alike — again.

Los Angeles, June 1, 2005

What Have We Reaped?

JOHN O'KEEFE **REAPERS,** ODYSSEY ENSEMBLE
THEATRE, LOS ANGELES, OPENED JULY 16, 2005

John O'Keefe

In the program notes for his new play, *Reapers*, playwright and director John O'Keefe describes the work as a "memory of a fantasy," "What in Greece was the island, in Iowa is the farm. The farmer is the king, his wife, the queen, his daughter, the princess, and his son, the prince. Joey Beam is the chorus. The storm has already happened. The play is being performed by ghosts."

Indeed, life down on the farm as presented by O'Keefe has as much in common with the Furies as it does with any Norman Rockwell portrait of a country family at table. For the Fox family, working a hardscrabble plot with nothing to farm but hay, everything has gone rotten before the play begins. Hulda, the mother, is catatonic, a wheelchair bound manikin her son describes as having been stuffed, but who from time to time awakens to terrorize all. Mildred Fox, the matriarch of this Orestesian brood, is a brutalized housewife longing to kill either her husband or her son, it doesn't seem to matter which. Her daughter Deirdre is a sometimes innocent but more often flirtatious young woman on the prowl. Son Bruce, whose major activities include raping the sleeping daughters of nearby families, nightly dueling with his father, and ultimately killing his best friend, characterizes his behavior as one of "startlement," an activity which consists mainly of popping out from beneath the bed of a young man, Tom O'Brien, whom the family has obtained from the state juvenile home to help with the three-day endurance test described as reaping. Locked in the basement between long stretches of hard work, Tom is subjected to homoerotic "startlements" by Bruce as well as the love-starved blandishments of Deirdre. The father is the kind of farmer my own Iowa grandfathers were, men who did little but work themselves into death.

As we observe this loving quintet at their evening chowdown ("dinner" is too polite a word), we witness their simple home-bound pleasures: washing their hands, chewing slices of white bread, and verbally abusing one other. Other than the nightly father-son fights in the barn, temporary escapes—the son's "running" with his friend Dickie, the daughter's quick forays into the local town for fresh admirers, the father's insistent consumption of alcohol, and the mother's brooding day and night-time visions—are the only possible "pleasures" available to them.

But there is no escape, obviously, for young Tom. He is their temporary prisoner, and as an outside agent caught in this spinning web of horror, is called upon to witness their unspeakable deeds and unwillingly participate in their disgusting visions and acts. At moments, O'Keefe brilliantly crystallizes the absurd but utterly logical political conclusions of right-wing America: it's time to stop allowing foreigners to come here and take over *our* jobs, and to start sending Americans overseas to destroy the foreigners' homes and cities and take over *their* jobs, *their* oil wells, *their* manufacturing plants.

The satire of this play, however, is at other times too broad. Religious fervor, racial prejudice, violent political values—the author has perhaps created too many vectors for this wacky, ultra-dysfunctional family to successfully embrace; and the final furor of nature, madness, and personal hate take the play to a mountaintop of hysteria that the wide-eyed audience can merely endure—all belief in and sympathy for its characters having long been erased.

The "hero" of this fantasy is nature itself, the forces that every farmer knows are at the center of his existence. Like O'Keefe, I grew up in Iowa. Even living in a city, as I did, the constant subject of daily life was the weather—there was never enough rain and there was always too much; it was always too hot, too cold. Every farm family had tales of relatives being killed by or surviving tornadoes.

The single-man chorus of this play, Joey Beam, poetically conjures up a world of just such forces—

clouds that shout, winds that whisper, earth that cries out from its daily abuse. And at the center of the horrible fury of this play are characters desperate themselves to sing out for the joy of living and the praise of nature's gifts. Deirdre and Tom both sing lovingly at moments in the play, and in one short scene, hidden away in her upstairs bedroom, the two remind one almost of another young couple, George Gibbs and Emily Webb of *Our Town*, discussing their lives and futures. We quickly realize, however, that, unlike the world facing the Thornton Wilder figures, the couple of this current-day fantasy have no real lives, no real future to embrace. Tom attempts to describe his family as a "broken" one, with a dead father and a mother who "forgets" him for long stretches in state orphanages and juvenile centers. Deirdre decries his metaphors as mere euphemisms. What is "broken" about a relationship where a mother refuses to retrieve him? The "relationship" is one of hostility, not a "break," which might suggest a possible mending. For, as she knows from her own insufferable life, there is no longer any hope for love. It may be that, given the "relationships" these would-be dreamers have had to endure, there is no longer even a possibility of hope. As the author describes the changing forces of nature in our real global-warmed world: "Diseases spread, spring arrives earlier, plant and animal range shift, the coral reefs bleach. There are downpours, heavy snowfalls, flooding, droughts and fires." Let us hope, O'Keefe seems to argue, that we awaken before the Apocalypse arrives.

Los Angeles, August 1, 2005

Reprinted from *The Green Integer Review*, NO. 1 (January–February 2006).

I have known John O'Keefe since 1998, when Mac Wellman and I included a play of his, All Night Long, *in the anthology* From the Other Side of the Century II: A New American Drama 1960-1995. *In 2003 I published his play* The Deatherians *in my Green Integer series, and I attended his drama about actors in Nazi Germany,* Times Like These, *at 2100 Square Feet in Los Angeles in October 2002. But I did not know until the announcement of the production of* Reapers *that, like I had, O'Keefe had grown up in Iowa. When I read of some of the play's themes and the fact that O'Keefe himself had lived as a young man in orphanages and juvenile homes, I began to fear that his farm-life experiences might be based upon a stay with one of my own relatives.*

I have an uncle still on a farm that, with its close proximity of to cattle to house, had horrified my assistant Diana Daves — who attended the performance reviewed above with me — traveling with me to visit my parents in that state. Diana and I had decided to stop by my uncle's farm. A storm was clearly brewing, and it looked like and smelled of a possible tornado. I was not sure of the way to my uncle's farm, but jokingly told her not to worry, that we could stop at almost any farm along the way and find a relative. We did just that, and sure enough, one of my uncle's brothers (and since my father's first cousin married by mother's sister, the man was my own second or third cousin) appeared at the door. "Good to see you, Dougie," he announced, peering round me in surprise at seeing a woman waiting in my car (I presume my being gay had spread to my country relatives by that time in my life). "Their farm is two intersections north and one intersection east," he answered my query about the location of Myron Zumbach's farm (the reader needs to know that nearly every square mile of Iowa is divided equally by roads — dirt, graveled, or blacktopped).

My own experiences upon youthful visits to that farm and the numerous other farms my uncles had once owned were highly unpleasant ones — in those days everyone worked (even visitors) in the fields to reap, pick the corn or detassel it. Accordingly, I was a little leery in asking O'Keefe where he had lived and the location of the farm mythologized in his play. The juvenile home was in Toledo — only a couple of counties away! We had immediately discovered, moreover, that we were both born in Waterloo! It appears, thank heaven, the farm upon which he was incarcerated was a bit further west. He graduated from Marshalltown, two counties east of where my sister lives today. My earliest years had been spent in Benton County, the county next door to his juvenile home.

Los Angeles, August 2, 2005

Something Wicked

ROBERT LONGO **SOMETHING WICKED THIS WAY COMES,** MARGO LEAVIN GALLERY, LOS ANGELES, SEPTEMBER 24–OCTOBER 29, 2005

ROBERT LONGO   *Untitled (Ophelia #7),* 2005

ROBERT LONGO
something wicked this way comes (Condor), 2005

In one of his few one-man American shows of the last several years, Robert Longo has again honed in on images that seem very appropriate to our time, in this case images of possible disaster and impending death. The large, delicately painted black and white sprays of water which represent the largest part of this new show center upon gigantically vertiginous waves that are at once things of great delicacy and beauty, but in their obvious power and frothèd white tentacles set against deeply black horizons cannot help but conjure up images that combine sex with power and, ultimately, disaster. These images were presumably painted before the terrifying TV images of hurricanes Katrina and Wilma, but they cannot but remind us of the dangerous forces of nature. The association of the show's name with witches and the power-hungry Macbeth, serve as perfect metaphor of how nature has seemingly turned upon us. In our country political figures, out of their own power-hungry motives (it costs money to enforce stricter conservation policies upon American industry and consumers) continue to doubt the existence of global warming. The result will be just such wrathful waves as these, waves not just of a rising ocean but of repeated action through time, waves of what we shall presumably have to suffer far into the future.

The same "mortal coil" is played out even more powerfully in Longo's sickeningly beautiful roses which, in their blood-red spirals look more menacing, in some ways, than a snake ready to strike. There is something pathologically sweet in their beauty. We can even smell, in our imaginations, their oversweet scent. Even if we were to be ignorant of all the thousands of legends of love and death wrapped up with these beautifully thorn-laden blooms, we would still sense in Longo's outsize depictions of these roses the scent of death — perhaps even a watery suicide like that of Ophelia. In that sense, the roses are simply another portrayal of the same deadly forces of nature seen in the waves. But strangely enough these petals appear in their condensed vortices stronger than the incoming waves of the other half of the show.

With their evocation of coiled beauty, vertigo, sex, and death, these paintings seem perfectly aligned with the images and concepts expressed in Alfred Hitchcock's movie *Vertigo*, and I suggested to Longo that it was too bad Hitchcock had not had him to depict the dream-sequence of roses in terrifyingly slow disintegration. The cartoon images Hitchcock used are perhaps the weakest feature of a movie that employed some of the same images as Longo did to arouse our primitive fears. Seeing this show just a few days after John O'Keefe's play *Reapers*—a work about some of these same issues—I wonder, indeed, what *have* we sown, and shall we reap?

Los Angeles, October 30, 2005

Reprinted from *The Green Integer Review*, NO. 1 (January–February 2006)

Longo's Empire

ROBERT LONGO, **EMPIRE,** THE CORCORAN GALLERY
OF ART, WASHINGTON, D.C. / 1981

My relationship with Robert Longo goes back several years. My companion Howard wrote one of the first essays on Longo in our *Sun & Moon: A Journal of Literature & Art* in 1979. Howard later presented a Longo retrospective at the Los Angeles County Museum of Art in 1989. In 1981, I reviewed Longo's great performance work, *Empire,* when it premiered in Washington, D.C.

Robert Longo

It is remarkable that the first complete performance of Robert Longo's *Empire* should have been mounted in Washington, D.C., a city which had witnessed relatively little performance art, but then, for a work as ambitious as this, the Corcoran's cavernous atrium was a perfect location. *Empire*'s three parts, *Sound Distance of a Good Man, Surrender* (previously performed at Washington's D.C. Space) and *Empire* reveal Longo at his romantic best. The scope of his work is Nietzschean, as Longo attempts to portray the history of human culture transformed from order through liberty into chaos, each stage characterized by a juxtaposition of image, music, and dance. The startlingly beautiful *Sound Distance* counterpoints a pedestalled classical soprano (Peggy Atkinson), a film of sculptured lion and man, and a "ballet," in which two males rotate in an adagio of ambiguous positions embracing sport, sexuality, and war. In *Surrender*, a "libertine" male and female slow-dance to Peter Gordon's taunting saxophone improvisation. And what is Longo's vision of chaos? Squinting through a smokescreen, the audience is "gunned down" fascistically by arching spotlights; row upon row of robotized waltzers dance out of the smoke.

An air-raid siren recalls the wail of the saxophone, engenders nostalgia for the shrieking human voice, and foretells the future.

Washington, D. C., 1981

Reprinted from *ArtXpress*, I, NO. 2 (1981)

About a year before this performance event, I had attended the premier, at D.C. Space, of Longo's Surrender. *Afterwards, Robert threw a large party, supplied with a great deal of liquor and drugs. Although I have long enjoyed the effects of liquor, I rarely have used drugs of any kind, and have only once or twice been affected by "pot." But here I smoked a couple of marijuana joints, without knowing that they had been laced with something else. Suddenly I was standing outside of myself looking in at my body! I was barely able to find my companion Howard and suggest we leave. "Shortly," he said. "Shortly." "I think we better leave now," I stuttered. "I can see myself!" The trip from downtown Washington, D.C. to College Park, Maryland, which usually takes about a half hour or less in good traffic, lasted for several days.*

Los Angeles, December 3, 2003

The Imperfect Medium

"THE PERFECT MEDIUM: PHOTOGRAPHY AND THE
OCCULT," THE METROPOLITAN MUSEUM OF ART, NEW
YORK, 27 SEPTEMBER–31 DECEMBER 2005.
CLÉMENT CHÉROUX, ANDREAS FISCHER, PIERRE
APPAXINE, DENIS GANGUILHEM, AND SOPHIE
SCHMIT, **THE PERFECT MEDIUM: PHOTOGRAPHY
AND THE OCCULT** (NEW HAVEN, CONNECTICUT: YALE
UNIVERSITY PRESS, 2005).

Eugène Thiébult, *Henri Robin and a Specter*

In November 2005 I saw "The Perfect Medium: Photography and the Occult" at the Metropolitan Museum of Art in New York. It was a fascinating show, and one that deserved the hour or so I spent staring at the photographs of supposed spirits, fluids, mediums, and supernatural matter.

Most of these images were obviously manipulated, beginning with the earliest works shown by the American William H. Mummler and the British photographers Frederick Hudson and John Beattie. Many of these represent subjects in reverie or half-asleep or at the medium's table with vague figures standing beside them or—occasionally, and almost comically, on their laps, as in the Frederick Hudson photo, "Alfred Russel Wallace with the Spirit of His Mother."

Some of these works were simple hoaxes, but others billed themselves as "phantasmagorical" entertainments, and indeed the works of Andre-Adolphe-Eugène Disdéri and Eugène Thiébult are quite frighteningly gory: the first photographer is represented with a set of photographs depicting two friends posing before the camera before one friend reappears (in a sequential image) naked with a helmet on his head, while the second photographer's "Henri

Robin and a Specter" of 1863 presents an image of a sheeted skeleton attempting to embrace a besuited gentleman in his study.

It took only a few years from these original images before the specters became less theatrical, allowing far more imaginative associations: the German photographer Theodor Prinz's "A Ghost," for example, shows three men at table with a white figure with no discernible features hovering above them. The American W. Fitz-Hugh Smith placed two blank "Seeds" plates upon a table in a semi-lighted room while two persons rested their hands upon them on five successive Friday nights. The results are two negatives representing a total of forty-two faces, Christ in the center of the first and Shakespeare at center of the second.

Frances Griffiths Elsie Wright of the United Kingdom depicted her young girls with miniature fairies and spites. Madge Donohoe, another Britisher, practiced what she called "skotography," photographs of spirits taken without a camera or light. Pressing a packaged photographic plate against her face at night, she "entered into communication" with "unseen operators"—most often her late husband or the detective writer Sir Arthur Conan Doyle (a great admirer of her work and that of other spiritualist photographers). Her prints represent rays of light surrounding circular images of individuals, masks of eyes, and other figures that appear to have natural forms.

The second part of the show was dedicated to manifestations of ectoplasm and fluids forming images and words, or sometimes simply swirling out the air of the mouths, noses, and other orifices of mediums and other seated figures. Perhaps the most disgusting of these are the photographs by the American R. W. Conant who pictured the medium Margery emitting masses of ectoplasm from her nose. Some mediums even produced ectoplasm in the likenesses of figures such as Arthur Conan Doyle, represented in a photograph by the Canadian Tomas Glendenning Hamilton.

Some photographers, such as Paul Le Cour lay claim to witnessing levitating tables and chairs. In the Dane Sven Türck's photographs of the 1940s, not only do chairs and tables go flying through space, but in at least one instance, the medium himself. The American Sorrat Group of the 1960s present colored snapshots of metal coffee tables and dolls rising above the ground, suggesting a comically gravity-free world of American domesticity.

Several of these photographers insisted upon witnesses to their activities and put heavy constraints upon their photographic processes to prove the "truthfulness" of their work. Today, of course, even the newspapers proclaim how easy it is—given the advent of the computer—to manipulate photographic images. But what we recognize in this show is that photography was always a medium that attracted manipulation of both image and audience—an important statement, I suggest, given the continued faith Americans (and, I am certain, citizens of other countries) put in photographic representation. It was almost inevitable that the two major works that attracted the ire of conservative politicians and religious leaders of the 1980s and 1990s were photographic images: the "Piss Christ" photographs of Andres Serrano and the nude images of black males by Robert Mapplethorpe—both of whom lost venues for their art and financial support. Had their works been paintings would they have caused the furor they evoked? Why should we so intertwine the photograph with a kind of realist presentation of life that it actually offends certain viewers? Of course, painting and sculpture can evoke the same reactions, but we understand, somehow, that *they* are "creations," evocations of experience and manipulations of reality, while we somehow "believe" in the photographic image. This show should certainly make us question that faith.

Perhaps this issue lies behind the images I find the most fascinating in this show: the "Thoughtography" of Ted Serios. In his mid-thirties, working as a elevator operator, Serios discovered that he could use his mind to project images onto film in an ordinary box camera. Drawing the attention of psychiatrist and psychical researcher Jule Eisenbud, Serios, overseen by researchers, underwent thousands of trials, witnessed by hundreds of different observers. The series is rather startling. There were more than four hundred works that contain specific images, some of these based on "target" figures concealed from Serios in various manners such as sealing the image in an opaque envelope. Although the correspondences to the "psychic" photographs were often not very close, it was sometimes the very differences which made these interesting. For example, in attempting to produce a picture of the Chicago Hilton Hotel, where he had once worked, Serios, with Eisenbud holding and triggering the camera some three feet away, produced instead the Hilton Hotel in Denver, but at an angle and perspective that would have been impossible for a photographer to accomplish — from a "position not achievable with an ordinary seven-foot stepladder but only with some special contrivance for getting the cameraman well into the air." In another so-called "distortion," Serios produced a photograph of Eisenbud's ranch outside of Denver without ever having visited it; even more strangely, however, was the fact that the ranch produced in Serios' thought-image did not represent the psychiatrist's ranch at the time of the event, but as it had been years earlier, without shutters on the windows and beside a barn in a condition in which it had never existed.

An alcoholic, Serios was not an easy subject, and one day he simply determined to stop the experiments. He seldom was able to mentally produce images again.

Many of us would like to believe in psychic phenomena: it would explain so many of our fantasies, our desires and dreams. But, in the end it is the imperfection of these images—the fascinating manipulation of reality that precludes belief—that makes them of interest to us as art.

Los Angeles, December 7, 2005

Answering the Sphinx

DAVID ANTIN, I NEVER KNEW WHAT TIME IT WAS
(BERKELEY: UNIVERSITY OF CALIFORNIA PRESS, 2005).

David Antin at his performance of
"california—the nervous camel"

I told my friend David Antin the other day that I had a bone of contention with his new book, *i never knew what time it was*. For the several days I was reading it, whenever I went into the room where I had last left his book and glimpsed the cover, I immediately began singing the Rodgers and Hart song. That song began to haunt me, in fact. I couldn't remember the actual lyrics, so I would begin with "I never knew what time it was / Till there was you..." and make up the rest... "What a strange time it was / so long without you," each time creating new lyrics. For those who have a memory for lyrics, of course, the song actually begins with the phrase "I *didn't* know what time it was / Till I met you." and continues, "Oh, what a lovely time it was, / How sublime it was too!" So both David (perhaps intentionally) and I had gotten the lyrics wrong. How appropriate for a book that is very much about memory, about what one *thinks* one remembers in relationship to whatever the *actual* "reality" may be.

Reading David's book, moreover, called up my own memories of David and his readings. I witnessed two of these pieces in their oral performances: "california — the nervous camel" at one of Paul Holdengräber's cultural forums at the

Los Angeles County Museum of Art—where I also served as unofficial photographer of the event—and "time on my hands," performed at CalArts. Accordingly, I spent some time, after reading these works, attempting to remember them in their oral manifestations—which seemed to me quite different from the written documents. This is inevitable, I suspect, when attempting to remember what was said during a hour-long event. In short, I experienced a sort of fracture between event and document, a sort "crack in time," if you will, which my memory had to bridge.

I have known David and his wife Eleanor now for about 25 years, moreover, and during that long period my personal memories of these and numerous other performances I've witnessed have become intertwined with their personal lives and the several events I shared with them.

For example, after reading "california—the nervous camel"—the title of which arose, apparently, from the travels of a San Diego couple to Egypt, where the couple's camera had captured the fall of a woman from a camel who'd been given contrary orders ("get up," "go down") by the camel driver—I could not quite comprehend this image within the context of what David was saying about the region. It was a wonderful image and *sounded* perfect as a metaphor for the desert lands of Southern California, but I grew uncertain whether California was like the camel because of the rolling earthquake-like temblors, the indecisiveness of its citizens or leaders, the quick rise and fall of its cultural interests and/or economy, or the constant shifts in its values. The metaphor presented a series of possibilities, all of which were of interest. Just as I had reinvented the lyrics of the standard ballad, I made a new meaning of David's image. I chose a much more personal meaning for the metaphor, picturing the author himself as the "the nervous camel"—albeit with *one* hump, that marvelously domed head that anyone who's seen him cannot forget.

When I first visited California, I stayed with the Antins, who lived, as they do today, near San Diego. I remember them picking me up at the train station and the three of us beginning a series of conversations that would continue seemingly non-stop during the two days of my visit. As he drove up the sandy paths to their then somewhat isolated home, David, speaking, seldom seemed to attend to the road, which terrified me! Between the continued movement of his hands and the almost complete inattention of his eyes upon the road, I was amazed we reached their house safely.

Later he took me to the beach—as he reminds me

it must have been the more isolated Solana Beach rather than the popular La Jolla beach—where I recall, with fondness, our remarkable discussion as we walked along the Pacific (in what must be one of the most beautiful landscapes in the world), his bald pate of his head glistening in the afternoon sun. We returned to the house and friends stopped by, friends who were introduced not just by name or vocation, but through extensive descriptions of their intellectual achievements and their current subjects of research. Such intense conversation is highly exciting, but also exhausting, and I was almost relieved to hit the bed. From my room across the way from their bedroom, however, I could hear David and Eleanor continuing the day's discussions long into the night. I realized that, in a sense, language never quite stopped in the Antin's house. Just as Eudora Welty had described the constant rhythm of the cotton gins as defining the life of the Fairchilds in *Delta Wedding*, so did the sound of voices define the Antins. It is easy for me, accordingly, to project the image of David as the nervous, one-humped camel of California, attempting to display the beauty of the landscape while discussing the narrative theory of my PhD dissertation which I was currently writing as we shuffled across the sand in a constant state of indecision between the enjoyment of space (sitting down to rest) and intellectual pleasure (moving forward with our ideas).

One might note that David was born into just such a world. As he describes his early life in his recent book-length conversation with Charles Bernstein: "My earliest family memories were living with my grandmother and my aunts—all beautiful women—living in a great old house in Boro Park. … People kept coming from all over the world to visit, to play cards or chess and to tell stories and argue in a handful of European languages about people and facts and politics. …And my grandmother presided over the entire household in a droll, mischievous manner. This is the household I most remember. It was noisy, cheerful and gay, and a world away from the austere prison of living with my mother, which happened only once in a while."

It is no wonder that Antin has spent a lifetime now "talking," talking in public about the past and family, the present and ideas, philosophy and reminiscences. Although Antin has long been determined to separate his "talking" from fiction or story, and has doggedly argued that his work, with its intense use of poetic devices, is *poetry*, one must admit—as David does finally in this new volume—that his is a life of storytelling as intense—if not as encyclopedic—as Scheherazade. Indeed, it is the life-saving necessity

of Scheherazade's *Thousand and One Nights*, a
necessity growing out of desire—in her case the
desire to survive—that most distinguishes Antin's
storytelling from other, more normative, patterns.

These, in fact, are the very subjects of this new book:
How does one remember? How does one understand
life within the constant flux of time? How does one
frame meaning when it constantly shifts? Or, to put
it in the context of "the nervous camel," how does
one live in a place that is simultaneously rising and
falling, beginning always anew by destroying the
old? Naturally, one cannot help tumbling from time
to time.

In exploring these ideas, however, Antin does not
simply weave fictions—at least the kind of fiction
most people understand by the word. For Antin's
talking is as interesting for what it leaves out as for
what it presents.

The long California piece, for example, is a strange
kind of love story. Well—it might be seen as a love
story, although we have no evidence, no plot details
that allow us any certainty. "california—the nervous
camel" is about many things, but at its heart is a
narrative about two couples, friends of the Antins,
who seemingly do everything—except travel on
vacation—together: Jack and Melissa, Richard and
Alexandra. When Jack is killed in a car accident,

Richard's behavior radically changes:

Richard never seemed to recover from jacks untimely accident
his life changed completely after that   he moved out of his house
 and into the servants quarters behind it   he stopped going to concerts
and openings   where alexandra appeared alone   he started spending
    more time at the clinic in mexico   and even that wasnt enough   for
a while he literally disappeared ...

but when he came back to
san diego he gave up his practice   left the house to Alexandra and
    took up an entirely new career....

In Antin's "story," in which the characters are not
overtly psychological, the reader/listener has no way
of knowing what Richard is really feeling. Perhaps
the death simply reminded him, as many men are
reminded at his age, of his own mortality; perhaps he
merely suffered a kind of mid-life crisis. Yet we feel,
given the extensiveness of his withdrawal from his
previous life, that the two men may have had a deeper
relationship than the narrative itself presents, that
perhaps their friendship might have been a gay one.
As with living beings, however, there is no discernable
"plot," we have no clear motivating action, just the
events, the *narrative* of his acts. Antin has presented
us with a story that, just as in my confusion of the
work of art and the person, creates a sort of "crack in

time" which the individual perceiver must fill with a significance of his own imagination. For Richard the face of the "nervous" camel, as it settled back into its relaxed state, appeared as a sphinx, an inscrutable beast demanding an answer to its impossible riddle, which is perhaps what Antin really means by his comparison of California to the camel. Clearly it is an image that might also help to describe Antin's art. For what the cracks or hollow spaces of Antin's "stories" force the reader to encounter is precisely that: the riddles of life.

In the title piece, Antin's father-in-law undergoes a stroke and is able to speak only one word that sounds as if it might be from his native language, Hungarian: *zaha*. "*zaha zaha* he said *zaha* shaking his head and repeating it over and over *zaha zaha* to anything we had to say." The Hungarian dictionary has no word remotely like it, and David is puzzled by the repeated word: is it a command? a desire? a person? something or someone he loved?

A Hungarian friend, a violinist, suggests it's an inverted word, *haza*, which means homeland. But even this "answer," if it is one, explains little. What does a dying man who has spent most of his life as a displaced Hungarian painter and poet in La Jolla mean by repeating "homeland?" As Antin notes:

…he was thinking of his homeland   and of course budapest is no longer his budapest   and keckemet is no longer the little town where his father painted the interiors of churches   but he was looking for this one place that he was sure never ever to find   again

The reader/listener can only imagine, can only fill in this "crack in time" with his own imaginative responses.

Something similar to the riddles at the heart of David's "stories" occurs also on their larger structural level. In the more constrained form of commercial fiction it is plot that carries forward the events. In other words, it is a pattern of narrative continuity that allows the specific events of a tale to occur at regular intervals to this:

Unhappy with her life, Jane takes a vacation to a small village to visit her friend Sally. There she meets an old friend Richard, a handsome man, who is still in love with her. Jane refuses the old friend's advances, but as she finds herself growing fond of him once again, she discovers that Sally, who has always hated Jane's husband, has secretly invited Richard to the town. At first she feels betrayed, but gradually comes to understand just how mistaken she has been in marrying her husband, a man whose affections she accepted just to goad her mother and father.

Suddenly, comprehending that her life has been lived in emptiness, she seeks out her old friend's love. But having been spurned twice, he has left the little country village. She follows him to the mountains, but he has moved on, and she is forced to return to her husband and family with the realization that true love will never be possible again. (If you don't like my hastily constructed plot, substitute the plot of almost any Henry James novel).

What Jane does in the little tourist town, the beautiful coat she wears as she again encounters Richard, what the town looks like, what she says to her acquaintances, the memories that overcome Jane in the little village — these are pearls on the string of the previous paragraph's somewhat banal story-line, that, apparently, retain the attention of certain kinds of passive readers.

In Antin's writing the strings have all been cut; his "tales" have no true beginning, no middle, no necessary end. Rather, they are structured by a sense of rhythm, most often linked by philosophical meditations or ideas, closing only when a literary narrative presents a parallel image of the ideas about which he has been talking.

For example, in "the noise of time" Antin begins with a discussion of an essay he'd read in *The Nation* on Robert Morris, an essay that disappoints the author and happens to mention the Hegelian aphorism that "an artwork is the embodiment of some truth." Antin finds it difficult to perceive something as tangible as a piece of art or an artwork as a receptacle for abstract concepts, propositions or ideas. Perhaps the closest an art work can come to the embodiment of an idea, he suggests, is in the form of a machine, as an example of which he drolly proposes a mousetrap, a killing machine set up to act in a certain way when the mouse licks the peanut-butter. But what if the mouse prefers jelly, or the spring on the trap was not properly wound, or a whole myriad of other events intervene? Will the machine-of-art still hold its truths? Perhaps the "truths" only work under certain conditions.

Abandoning this possibility, Antin humorously explores another, slightly violent image: perhaps making art is more like bowling. The ideas are the pins toward which one propels the work of art, the ball of art hitting some of them, leaning against others. But the author admits he is a terrible bowler and most of his balls reach only the gutter. How does one then get at ideas through art? How does something mean?

Ultimately Antin argues that, for him, a work of art is something in which ideas go running in all directions, sometimes to be lost, sometimes accidentally crossing paths with others. He presents two narratives to prove his point about how ideas are lost or are transformed into other things. Having just purchased a copy of the Russian poet Osip Mandelstam's essays, *The Noise of Time*, he is struck with the translator's use of the word "noise" in the title, since in Russian *shum* is used to evoke the sound of repetitive or abrasive events, "the rustle of leaves," "the roar of the sea," "the pounding of the surf," "the clamor of a crowd," etc. Translating Pushkin's *Eugene Onegin*, Vladimir Nabokov renders the word as "hubbub." Why has this translator, Clarence Brown, translated the word as "noise?" Perhaps, argues Antin, Brown was influenced by the period in which he was translating, when "noise" came to be understood as entropy, "the growing disorder that affects all ordered systems over time the frictional forces that reduce all directed energies to forms of disorder sooner or later as we go from more orderly universes to more disorderly universes given enough time." I am personally somewhat skeptical about this explanation for the translator's choice, but certainly anyone aware of the association of the word "noise" with "entropy," would find the title much richer, as Antin argues, than Mandelstam might ever have imagined in his use of *shum*. And that is Antin's point. Time and its myriad changes alter the way in which we interpret things, even *how* we interpret.

Perhaps a more convincing example is a discussion he has with the critic Leo Steinberg about a passage of Shakespeare's *Measure for Measure*. Steinberg uses the passage as a proof of Shakespeare's genius: "His head sat so tickle on his shoulders that a milkmaid might sigh it off an she had been in love." For Steinberg, the choice of the word "tickle" so close to a dark moment when the hero is in danger of losing his life, is proof of the bard's monumentality. Antin, however, is suspicious. Perhaps the word "tickle" meant something other in Shakespeare's day than the light rubbing under the arms, something we have forgotten. Looking it up later in the OED, Antin finds that indeed it had been used in a fifteenth century text to describe rocks "that stood tickle in a stream," rendering passage perilous. His inclination is to write Steinberg, telling him of the discovery, that the older meaning has simply been lost in "the noise of time." But he resists doing so, knowing that he would simply take away Steinberg's great delight in the "strange" usage of the word. In short, the "truth" of the meaning is of less interest than the reinterpretation of it.

This "story's" final narrative event concerns the same father-in-law he describes in his title piece. Antin's then teenage son Blaise and the poet from

Hungary enjoyed one another's company, played tennis together, discussed literature and even, apparently, the older man's "Schnitzlerian" love life in the old days of Budapest and Vienna, which must have reflected his present sexual loneliness, with which Blaise could probably sympathize, coming as he was into his full adolescence. But Blaise was about to go away to college, and desiring to give his grandfather a special gift, he and a friend came up with the idea of setting him up with a hooker, which they planned to do with what they perceived to be the quite generous sum of $150. All the hooker had to do is to pretend to accidentally encounter the gentleman and seduce him. "you don't have to say a lot," the boys explained, he may just show you his paintings and "recite some poetry to you." They tried several street girls but found no hooker willing to take on the job, not if they had to listen to poetry!

What Antin reveals in this wonderful narrative is the absolute worthlessness of poetry and art as a container for good ideas. The gap between generations has been bridged by his son's and his father-in-law's friendship, but what I have called "the cut in time" has irreparably severed the art from its would-be perceivers, for the art—and whatever truths it may bear—has no currency in the world of these women of the street.

In this "talk," as in almost all of Antin's "stories," there is no true plot, but a series of events or narrative incidents that can only be comprehended—if they can truly *be* comprehended—through the reader's/listener's imagination, his desire to make meaning and determination to answer the sphinx.

Isn't that, of course, what all great art, all great poetry and fiction depends upon—the willingness of the author to invite the reader into the text and the reader's reciprocation? After all, Scheherazade would not have been able to relate her remarkable stories if the Caliph had refused to listen.

Los Angeles, July 25, 2005

Reprinted from *The New Review of Literature*, Vol. 3, no. 2 (April 2006).

The Necessary Remedy

JANE BOWLES (WITH MUSIC BY PAUL BOWLES) **IN THE
SUMMER HOUSE,** PLAYHOUSE THEATRE, NEW YORK,
DECEMBER 29, 1953

THE PLAY WAS REVIVED AT THE VIVIAN
BEAUMONT THEATRE OF THE LINCOLN CENTER,
NEW YORK, AUGUST 1, 1993, (INCIDENTAL MUSIC BY
PHILIP GLASS)

Jane Bowles

It was the year of Queen Elizabeth's coronation, the year that saw the first color television set, the great flood in the North Sea and "great" tornadoes in Michigan (the storms killing more than 200 people). The Platters and The Four Tops began their musical careers. The year saw the deaths of two great theater legends, Eugene O'Neill and Lee Shubert (one of the three legendary Shubert brothers). Broadway saw productions of Tennessee Williams' *Camino Real*, Arthur Miller's *The Crucible*, and Leonard Bernstein's *Wonderful Town*. I was six years of age. Despite all these facts and my long-standing conviction that the 1950s is today a highly misunderstood decade — more sophisticated than we imagine it today — I am still trying to comprehend what it must have been like to encounter Jane Bowles' play that year of 1953, which ran for only 55 performances on Broadway.

The play actually had a history that went back to the late 1940s. Bowles' friend Oliver Smith evidently had been trying to convince Jane to write a play for several years, and in 1946 and 1947, in Vermont and Paris, she wrote much of the play, the first act of which was published in *Harper's Bazaar* in 1947. In 1951 the play was performed at the Hedgerow Theater in Moylan, Pennsylvania, with Miriam

Hopkins in the lead. Just before the Broadway production, Jane's husband Paul came from Morocco to New York and wrote music for the work, seeing it through rehearsals and production.

How could actors and audiences of that time be prepared for such a work? Bowles' writing is so original that it is hard to compare it with any other writer of the day—or perhaps even now. The expressionist and fantastic aspects of Tennessee Williams' *A Streetcar Named Desire* might be described as the work closest in tone to Bowles' play. Williams, in fact, was a close friend of Jane's. Bowles' work, however, is far more comically surreal than even the most "campy" of Blanche's observations in Williams's 1947 production.

If Paul Bowles is to be believed, it is clear that the lead actor of the play, the great Judith Anderson, did not know what to make of the character. "Who am I? Who am I supposed to be?" she often asked in her frustrated interruptions of rehearsals. Evidently even the onstage psychoanalyst could not answer her. No one seemed to understand what the play was about.

Bowles herself clearly wanted actors that could play their roles in the grand manner of highly theatrical performance. She hand-selected both Judith Anderson for the role of Mrs. Eastman Cuevas and the divine Mildred Dunnock for Mrs. Constable. A young actor named James Dean was rejected for the lesser role of Lionel because he was too "normal."

For Bowles narrative does not function in a traditional manner. There is no straightforward "plot" to this play, nor any of the tightly knit interconnecting patterns of scenes and acts that make up most so-called Broadway plays. Indeed the set changes in every scene of Act One—as it moves from a garden in Southern California to the beach and back to the garden—and Act Two, which occurs in the nearby popular restaurant. The characters shift focus throughout, as the major figure of Act I disappears—along with numerous other characters, including husband, sister-in-law, her daughter, and servants—from the very center of the play. Casual figures such as Lionel, whom we first encounter carrying an advertising placard displaying Neptune, become central characters. A young girl who appears briefly in two scenes (becoming a victim of either accident or murder) is "replaced" by her mother, who ultimately becomes perhaps the central figure in the play. A restaurant worker—Jean Stapleton in the original production—is later introduced, becoming an important voice of the second act. In short, the play moves forward through a near structureless series of "surprises," twists, and turns in characters, plot, and meaning.

It is the emotional states of its figures that drive this work forward—and, at times, backward. Act One establishes the central character's role and symbolic position immediately as Gertrude Eastman Cuevas stands upon the balcony of her beach home calling to her daughter below: "Are you in the summer house?.... Are you in the summer house?" wherein her daughter indeed has sequestered herself. Although she is front and center in the scene, Mrs. Eastman Cuevas is equally removed from all, even from the man whom she admits she may marry, Mr. Solares, who soon enters with sister, her daughter, and servants in tow. The comical picnic that follows—with Solares and family in the garden, Gertrude on the balcony, and Molly hidden away—sets the tone of the entire work: absurdity, imperiousness, humility, and complete acceptance of all of these are its matter.

Solares, the courtier of the haughty Mrs. Eastman Cuevas, politely attempts to present the strange scene as one of normality, while his sister, Esperanza, crudely pokes holes in the pretense of both. When Mrs. Eastman Cuevas expresses her love of the ocean, Esperanza declares that she "hates it." When Gertrude (believing her first husband was not sufficiently interested in his job) asks Solares if he likes his work, Esperanza interrupts: "He don't like no business—he likes to stay home and sleep—and eat." Later, upon Gertrude's disapproval of such a heavy meal in the middle of the day, the overweight Esperanza quickly catalogues the heavy breakfasts and lunches she and her family consume: "For breakfast: chocolate and sugar bread: for lunch: soup, beans, eggs, rice, roast pork with potatoes and guava paste…Next day: soup, eggs, beans, rice, chicken with rice and guava paste—other day: soup, eggs, beans, rice, stewed meat, roasted baby pig and guava paste. Other day: soup, rice, beans, grilled red snapper, roasted goat meat and guava paste." So much for normality!

Enter Lionel and friends bearing placards of Neptune and a mermaid to advertise the local restaurant, The Lobster Bowl. Molly, called out of her hideaway to give them water, is delighted by the marvel of their costumes, and Lionel, clearly attracted to her, gives her a little plastic lobster as a gift. As if the stage were not filled enough as it was with its strange assortment of characters, Gertrude's new lodger, Vivian, suddenly appears. She is as enthusiastic and excitable as Esperanza has been sarcastically honest. As quickly as she is whisked away into the house, her mother, Mrs. Constable, appears, worried about her overwrought daughter's mental health.

In short, within a single scene Bowles has spilled 14 characters onto the stage—all but one in the play—expressing their various emotional states as if midway through a grand opera. And, in this sense, no further scenes can quite compare with the play's first. The rest of the work, scene by scene, explores the various relations between these bigger-than-life figures.

Scene Two presents Molly one month later, temporarily out of hiding, as she encounters the vivacious and avaricious Vivian skillfully attempting to take her place in the hearts of both Gertrude and Lionel. The scene ends with Gertrude, Solares and his extended family, and Mrs. Constable in search of her beloved "bird." The audience can only suspect what—through her slightly hysterical interrogations of her daughter—Gertrude clearly also suspects, that Molly has pushed Vivian over the cliff.

Scene Three, one month later, presents the aftermath (celebration is an incorrect word) of the double weddings of Gertrude and her daughter. As the women each prepare to leave their homes and face separation, with neither one seeming to perceive any future with her new husband, the dramatic attention shifts to the drunken Mrs. Constable, who, with her daughter's death and no other purpose in life, has stayed on in the beach community. The interchange between these strong women, where Mrs. Constable expresses her preference for the sharp-tongued truth-teller Mrs. Lopez over the imposing bitch-liar she perceives in Mrs. Eastman Cuevas, presents a stunning encounter between a being who struggles to keep in control and another who has freed herself from nearly all constraints. It is as comical as it is shocking.

Act II, made up of two scenes, is nearly emptied of the first act's dramatic force. The Lobster Bowl, where Lionel works, has become merely another "summer house" for Molly, as she passes the time with card games and reading and rereading her mother's letters from Mexico. The witty interchanges between Inez, waitress in the restaurant, and Mrs. Constable are what saves these dark and dreary scenes from bringing the play to a near standstill. Yet, the play does begin to unwind, and Lionel, recognizing the need for change, suddenly becomes courageous enough to demand that he and Molly move away to St. Louis, where his brother is involved in selling barbecues. The hilarious irony of his shift from boiler to barbie is almost lost in the darkly comic, but often wise, discussions between Mrs. Constable and Molly, and the older woman's attempts to convince her to follow Lionel, to escape the dark confines of her life.

Molly, however, has word that her mother is returning, and she awaits her arrival with joy and consternation. Her mother's entry and her declarations of the horrible (and to the viewer/reader, hilarious) life with the family in Mexico merely point up her selfishness. She is happy nowhere, neither on the balcony of the vine-covered beach house nor the highly peopled rooms of her husband's abode. Now nearly powerless, she is must again find someone she can control. But just as the view of the garden was altered with her mother's departure, so does her mother now seem changed in Molly's perception. As her mother desperately tries to rein in her daughter by telling Mrs. Constable that Molly killed Vivian (which, interestingly enough, Mrs. Constable denies), Molly suddenly recognizes that she must escape, that she must leave with Lionel. Mrs. Eastman Cuevas, like Mrs. Constable, is left without a purpose, almost a child again herself, recalling some horrible unnamed event that we suspect was probably centered around an attempt to gain love.

Without wishing to sound as if I have undergone too many viewings of *The Wizard of Oz* (a movie, I admit, I saw again quite recently), I might suggest that Bowles's characters could be compared with the three friends of Dorothy in search of a heart (Mrs. Eastman-Cuevas), a brain (Mrs. Constable), and courage (Lionel) in order to save the young heroine from the mistakes of their lives. The poignant conversation between Mrs. Constable and Molly near the end of the play point up the problems of nearly everyone involved in Bowles' fantastical journey.

Warned in her mother's letters not to dream, Molly is nearly ready to give up her life and submit again to her mother's control. "Why shouldn't you dream?" asks Mrs. Constable (I can hear Mildred Dunnock's voice in the very question). "I used to waste a lot of time day-dreaming," answers Molly. "Why shouldn't you dream? Why didn't she want you to?" Mrs. Constable persists. "Because she wanted me to grow up to be wonderful and strong like she is," responds the young girl. Mrs. Constable and we, the audience, know that her mother—having abandoned all dreams—is neither wonderful nor strong. Like Vivian at the cliff, the balcony is merely a height from which one can easily fall. And so too is the ephemeral surf Mrs. Constable prefers—the foam on her face that makes her believe, momentarily, that life is beginning once more—insufficient to help one go on living. The needs of the heart and mind alone are never enough. One must have the courage to act. As Lionel puts it, the longer one puts off acting the harder it is to do so. "Suppose I kept on closing that door against the ocean every night because the ocean made me sad and then one night I went to open it and I couldn't even find the door. Suppose I couldn't tell it apart from the wall any more. Then it would be too late and we'd be shut in here forever once and for all." Jane Bowles describes the necessary remedy simply as a stage direction: Molly's *flight is sudden*.

Los Angeles, July 14, 2005

Living Darwinism

EDWARD ALBEE **SEASCAPE,** THE SHUBERT THEATRE,
NEW YORK, JANUARY 26, 1975
REVIVED AT THE BOOTH THEATRE, NEW YORK,
NOVEMBER 2005. (THE PRODUCTION I WITNESSED
WAS A MATINEE PERFORMANCE ON NOVEMBER
6, 2005)

TEXT: EDWARD ALBEE **SEASCAPE,** (NEW YORK:
DRAMATISTS PLAY SERVICE, 1975).

Edward Albee

A retired married couple, Nancy and Charlie, are enjoying a seaside beach. She is painting; he, resting on a nearby blanket. The only interruption of their obvious pleasures is the roaring of a jet plane.

We soon discover, however, that other less pleasurable issues lie just below the surface. Nancy enjoys the day so thoroughly that she would like to "stay [on the beach] forever!" She loves the water, the air, the sand, the dunes, the beach grass, and the sunshine, and imagines the possibility of moving from beach to beach, going "around the world and never leav[ing] the beach…" The more practical Charlie scoffs at the notion. But she persists: it's necessary to find out what he really likes and "make all the plans." But Charlie, clearly, prefers doing nothing, just vegetating: no planning for enjoyment is in his view of the short future they may have left.

So Albee's Pulitzer Prize-winning play *Seascape* begins. It's a small spat, a typical domestic debate, and on one level the play never seems to rise above this—the small, domestic issues of a healthy but slightly aging couple attempting to determine what to do with their future. Even the sudden appearance of a couple of marvelously colored lizards curious about these beachside interlopers doesn't move the play far off topic: for the lizards not only speak fluent English, but they, too, are a monogamous couple attempting to determine what the future holds in store.

Despite some moments of terror, some suggestions of dark horror, and a great deal of humor as the two "animals" and two "humans" attempt to comprehend each other's worlds, the play seems, as *New York Times* reviewer Ben Brantley wrote of the production I recently saw, to "lack emotional gravity," to be perfectly likeable but also, in some way, "forgettable"—particularly in the context of Albee's more highly emotionally pitched *oeuvre*. In some respects, I agree. There is a problem at the heart of this play that relates to the text's seeming insistence on a kind of realist fantasy. The lizards who seem ready to climb out of their watery domain into a Darwinian transformation seem too glibly linked by their author to their human counterparts; the humans, in turn, seem too ready to embrace them, to understand their dilemmas and even *help* them adapt to the brave new world they are about to enter. The human couple insist that there is no way for the lizards to return to the sea: "You'll have to come back…sooner or later. You don't have any choice."

And we clearly recognize that the final lines of the play, the male lizard Leslie's challenge to their offer of help: "All right. Begin." is a hollow one, since the humans cannot even agree on to handle the issues facing their own lives. Should they act out a kind of desperate series of adventures to temporarily stave off what is soon to be their fate or should they, as Charlie's actions suggest, curl into an eternal nap?

Part of the problem that arises in the current production is that the wonderfully able actress Frances Sternhagen may not have the best choice for the role of Nancy. In the original play the role was performed by Deborah Kerr, and, although I never saw that production I can imagine the kind of plucky common sense (witnessed in Kerr's role as a nun in *Heaven Knows, Mr. Allison*) and the slightly romantic and dreamy figure (as she played in *The King and I*) that might allow the mix of reality and fantasy so necessary in this work. Sternhagen plays the role, rather, as a kind Connecticut do-gooder against George Grizzard's curmudgeonly city-dweller, and the mix doesn't allow the play to slip into the metaphoric dimension into which it seems naturally to want to expand.

I think Albee is not at all interested in the redemption of two bestial creatures, but in the possible redemption of a human couple's life. As Charlie points out, it would be impossible to recount to anyone their conversation with two lizards. The lizards are, after all, not "real" but phantasmagorical mirror images of the couple themselves. Charlie's own childhood activity of standing and sitting for long periods at the dark bottom of bodies of water is paralleled by the former activities of their lizard counterparts. In short, he has always had the predilection to return to a beast-like state. On the other hand, Nancy, not unlike the giant birds the lizards recognize in the passing airplanes, is almost ready to fly away in her own extended visions of possibility. In order to live life to its fullest does one have to chase the future until, utterly exhausted, one falls into one's grave? To be an actively living species does it necessarily mean one has to embrace every possible Darwinian change?

The vision this human couple share, that they indeed are not very different from the beasts from which their kind sprang, is, perhaps, an obvious one, even a fairly likeable conclusion (if you're not a religious fundamentalist)—but it is not, to repeat Brantley's phrase, "forgettable," or at least it *should not* be forgettable. For it is that vision that leads us to these very questions and the solutions necessary for the successful continuation of our lives. If war between the sexes and between generations is the subject of many of Albee's dramas, it is the possibility of peace that he here proposes. We have to help one another, he implies, to *begin* living the human potentiality of our lives.

Los Angeles, November 25, 2005

Singing the Body Electric

MATI UNT **THINGS IN THE NIGHT**, TRANSLATED
FROM THE ESTONIAN BY ERIC DICKENS (NORMAL,
ILLINOIS: DALKEY ARCHIVE PRESS, 2006).

Mati Unt

The Estonian writer Mati Unt published his fiction *Öös on asju* in 1990, and Dalkey Archive has just released an English translation by Eric Dickens of this masterwork, *Things in the Night*.

Rather than a novel, the work might be described as a kind of loosely knit fictional journal covering a certain period of the author/narrator's life and Estonian history. The central figure undergoes a series of rather unpleasant and interrelated events, all connected in some way with his secret hobby, a passion for electricity. And, indeed, the fiction holds together like a series of positive and negative ions ready to take on an electric charge. There are approximately eight "events" that make up the substance of this book.

Unt begins with sections from an uncompleted novel focused on a young, disaffected Estonian (not unlike himself) who has decided that instead of committing suicide he will endeavor to perform an immediate deed that will wake up the world and, possibly, make it temporarily a better place. Determined to blow up a small electrical station in Liikola, the character, we perceive, is a comic one, who recognizing his own ridiculousness, still hopes, as he puts it, to at least go out "with a bang. Or at least make a fool of myself, such a great fool of myself, such a fool that people would snicker for a hundred years to come... The man wanted to blow up machines here in Northern Europe, wanted to become a new Luddite, a new Herostratus: naïve, but justified in his actions; crazy, but interesting, banal, but a man of his time...." The figure, however, falls to sleep instead, and upon awaking, realizes just that the plan alone is perhaps enough. He throws his rucksack full of weapons into a river and returns home. So too does the author realize that he has no novel to write. The book is left halfway finished—although part of it is published in a local newspaper.

The second "event" is the author's encounter with a young woman, Susie, who with the narrator leaves a party and freely gives herself in sex, proclaiming the next morning that she is determined to have a child with him. The narrator is appalled and quickly escapes what he sees as the woman's "assault."

In a third such "event," a woman delivers to the narrator 100 or so cacti, evidently moving in with them for a period of time. This woman remains quite shadowy throughout the book, but apparently the narrator has a longer relationship with her; clearly the cacti remain in his possession.

A fourth "event" occurs as the hero determines to go mushroom hunting, even though he knows clearly it is not yet the right time of year. In the forest where he has been left by a taxi, he becomes impossibly lost, and, more and more disoriented as he proceeds, he nearly gives up. Suddenly other hikers appear, and ultimately he finds his way back to Tallinn, recognizing that he is near the home of his friend, the noted Estonian explorer, documentary author and filmmaker, Lennart Meri (who, in the real world, would ultimately become the Foreign Minister of Estonia in the period between the fall of the Soviet Republic and Estonian freedom in 1990-1991). The pleasant conversation between himself and Meri is interrupted by the appearance of a gnome-like shaman, an old woman patiently sitting in a nearby chair. Upon leaving this noted figure's house, the narrator hides, witnessing the appearance of two other such old women, dressed in black. As he waits even longer, another seems to appear—the mystery of which sends him running off.

On his way home, his taxi is stopped by the police who have cordoned off a street where, it appears, they have captured a cannibal who has been the subject of various stories passing throughout the city for months. The narrator observes the cannibal as he sits on Yablochkov Street, his hands tied behind his back.

A visit from an old school friend, Tissen, results in a long series of monologues about problems facing the world and, in particular, Estonia. Although the narrator attempts to enter the one-sided conversation, he is quickly shut up, as he is forced to listen to vague descriptions of Tissen's scientific project and his threats of "something big to come."

On New Year's Day, the narrator's birthday, the city suddenly loses its power and for that day and the next there is a ghastly silence over the city as a cold storm blows through. The city remains without heat or light. The narrator leaves his home, eventually, in the ice-cold air, encountering another being who tells him of events—including the Communist party's attempts to solve the crisis. As the narrator returns home, he encounters a vision of Susie on the stairwell, now a kind of feminine deity who cuts off his head. He awakens in a hospital, having suffered erysipelas or "rose-face," an infection that spreads through the lymphatic vessels resulting in streaking of the face, fever, chills and pain.

The narrator is later told that the power failure was due to his friend Tissen's "Conscience" machine, which overloaded the transformers and might have caused an outage over the whole of Europe. Because of his own writings about just such a figure and his friendship with Tissen, the narrator is suspected of being involved with Tissen's acts, but ultimately is found innocent—innocent of knowledge and act.

If these "events" seem unrelated and fragmentary, they are presented as such. What connects them is a series of recurring images, themes, and issues that create within the text a kind of 'Ring Cycle"-like coherency: images of pigs, mushrooms, cacti, destructive and disenchanted beings, darkness and light, and all things connected with electricity from "the body electric" of Whitman to lightning and other electric discharges, fields of electrical forces, the "electric" relations between human beings, etc. There is, indeed, a kind of energy to this book that is not unlike that of the "Ring Cycle," the Walsung-like Estonian folk desperately seeking out the "ring" in the form of the power of electricity, with all of its positive and extremely negative consequences, the narrator serving as a kind of oafish Siegfried—a hero without a true battle to fight.

But what most strikes the reader of this fiction is not so much the events I have outlined above, but the relationship *between* those events, the often comic and yet terrifyingly consequential effects of the seeming series of plots, not one of which is complete in itself. A novel is begun and left unfinished; a woman desires a child from a man who believes the world is already overpopulated; a man is lost and then found; a great world figure is perhaps consorting with magic; an enemy of the people is captured; a scientist reveals some of his mad secrets; a dire catastrophe is narrowly averted. Like a series of outlines for various fictions, Unt's "events" become fascinating because of their multiple linkings, the numerous *possibilities* of meaning: there is no one solution, no one meaning proffered.

Unlike Wagner's great series of operatic events, moreover, Unt's work ends in a sort of redemption, as the light plays across the simple beauty of the landscape. Despite the desire and need of humans to get involved in some way in the various events of the day—small and large, comic and tragic—there is also a *Candide*-like possibility of tending one's own garden. "We could be as free as pigs who ran in the fields. Those were beautiful years, beautiful autumn days."

In this fascinating recounting of the dark final years of Estonia's Communist rule, we recognize that Unt had an enormous talent for revealing the human side of history, and it is sad to know that he died this past August at the age of 61.

Los Angeles, November 28, 2005

(Reprinted from *The American Book Review*, Vol. 27, no. 4 (May/June 2006)

The recent death of Lennart Meri (March 14, 2006) seems a sad occasion. As I've noted above, Meri appears as a major figure in Unt's novel. Reading of his activities — he was not only a politician, but an historian and filmmaker — I was reminded of my visit to Estonia in November 1989, during the very days when Estonia, along with Lithuania and Latvia, declared economic independence from the Soviet Union. I was touring with the ROVA Saxophone Quartet on their second trip to the Soviet Union and Baltic countries. Traveling

with the group were several poets and friends, including Clark Coolidge and his wife, and Lyn Hejinian, whose husband Larry Ochs is one of the group's founders. Meri would come to power as the foreign minister the following year, and was obviously deeply involved with Estonian politics during my two-day visit.

Tallinn was a sort of wild city in those days. It had been noticeable after visiting then-dreary, winter-besieged Leningrad (now St. Petersburg), that the Baltic countries were better off. The hotels were modern, the streets filled with activity. Tallinn, I felt, was the most beautiful of the three cities we visited in countries on the Baltic, which included Vilnius and Riga. But Tallinn was also a very strange place because it had long served during the Soviet years as a kind of cheap tourist dump—a source of inexpensive liquor and sex—for the Finns and Swedes, who would take the day boat, stay overnight in one of the two major hotels, and return the next afternoon—drunk out of their minds and, presumably, sexually satisfied. We were staying at one of those hotels.

Clark Coolidge had noticed early on in the day something unusual was in the air. "I feel like I did back in high school," he noted. "It feels creepy, like I'm surrounded by all these toughs." As we sat in the hotel dining room on the top floor of the building, eating our dinner, we began to notice the arrival of several tall, *burly men. The lights were dimming, and the large mirrored ball hanging from the ceiling seemed to have dropped. The magical hour when the dining room became a disco was fast approaching, and we perceived we had better quickly finish up. Our group was rather tightly knit and we enjoyed one another's company. However, a young woman from Berkeley, a lesbian activist, who had evidently broken up with her lover the day before she left on this trip, was a bit out of place among the rest of us middle-aged travelers. She was having emotional difficulties, and she turned to me quite often in her despair, in part because I am gay, which she assumed made me sympathetic. This particular evening, as we rose en masse to leave, a very large Finnish man who reminded me of Wagner's Hafner blocked one of our paths. "Out of the way," our young lesbian shouted! Hafner intently stood his ground, more out of shock I suspect than out of any evil intention.*

In what today may seem a rather sexist gesture, but which at the time I enacted as a reflex of self-protection, I lifted her up and gently put her down in a nearby aisle. As we moved forward in that new direction, I whispered: "In Tallinn, we do not argue with strangers." Later, I was to compare that late-night disco with the famous bar of international freaks presented in Star Wars.

Another rather hilarious event occurred in Tallinn the very next day. I was fascinated in the Soviet Union and in the Baltic countries by the incoherence of the merchant shops. I visited numerous stores in Russia, Lithuania, Latvia, and Estonia—something I would never do in the USA, where I am known as someone who hates shopping. But on this trip, the whole group had dubbed me "the shopper." I rarely bought anything, since there was often little to buy in these places. In Latvia, a jewelry store, for example, featured only tumbling mats on the day I visited—hundreds of tumbling mats! In Tallinn, the stores looked quite cosmopolitan, but were often closed because of lack of merchandise. One clothes shop, however, was open, and I entered. By this time I had figured out what size shirts and pants I might fit into, since there were seldom but one or two sizes, and one would never have been given opportunity to try anything on. I wandered through the store, suddenly spotting a pile of quite lovely shirts that seemed to be exactly my size. I picked one of the shirts up, discovering that the price was about the equivalent of 35 cents—how could I resist? But by this time, I caught the gazes of some of the Estonian shoppers, who, I am sure, were wondering what an American was doing in a clothes store in Tallinn. Had I lost my mind? In those days everyone knew in Tallinn that there is nothing—save sex and alcohol—to be bought! A cry was uttered, and suddenly from everywhere in the store, it seemed, women came running, grabbing at the same pile of shirts before which

I'd stood. I lost my balance and found myself among their legs on the floor of the establishment. I had caused a near-riot of purchasing frenzy. I still have that shirt, now a little bit frayed at the collar.

Los Angeles, March 20, 2006

Borders Without Borders

The book by Mati Unt, moreover, was not the first book of Estonian fiction that I had reviewed. In 2000, when I was planning a review and guide of the books of that year, I had written on Tõnu Õnnepalu's novel, Border State. *This review is previously unpublished.*

TÕNU ÕNNEPALU **BORDER STATE,** TRANSLATED FROM THE ESTONIAN BY MADLI PUHVEL (EVANSTON, ILLINOIS: NORTHWESTERN UNIVERSITY PRESS, 2000).

The narrator of Õnnepalu's excellent short novel *Border State* claims to live in a world without borders or where borders are meaningless. Born in the so-called border state of Estonia, which shares actual borders with Russia and Latvia and speaks a language similar to that of Finland, the narrator tells the story of his life while in Paris in halting French. "All geography is just a dream, a fantasy," he claims. "In reality, all countries have become imaginary deserts of ruins where crowds of nomads roam from one attraction to the other, sweeping over nations, skipping like fleas from continent to continent." But in truth he is deluded, a delusion responsible for his murdering his wealthy male lover.

For the contrite and philosophic narrator of *Border State* encounters "borders" almost wherever he goes, and actual blockades in his attempts to blend into and be assimilated into the new European society he encounters. His own past, lived in the dark and bleak cold of the Estonian world, has also imbued him with a sense of deprivation, particularly during the Soviet control and occupation of his country. Although neither narrator or author speak of politics, it is clear that the years of hardship have taken their toll on him and his people; like Péter Nádas's character in his great novel *A Book of Memories*, the experiences of a closed world of secrecy and fear have transformed utterly the people suffering those conditions. While he can only embrace the wealth and beauty of the Paris shops and homes, and he often speaks negatively of his birthplace, there is also a great love and longing for his country. His inability to be express this longing and embrace this love further accentuates his own consciousness of difference and cripples his abilities to openly love anything or anyone. Raised by a "grandmother" who was really his mother's stepmother from Poland, the narrator has grown to adulthood surrounded by old age and imminent death. He and his lover alike speak of his homeland as if it were a strange outpost to which no sane person could want to return, and that rejection translates into a personal one as well. In short, he is himself a border state, a man who both hates and loves his own past, who desires the west but recognizes its often hollow and crass aspects. As he tells his story to Angelo—an imagined stranger, an angel, an other self—he exists in a condition between sanity and madness, innocence and absolute guilt. Just as his credit card runs out, so too does his spiritual "credit," and he has no choice but to return to the desolate and cold world which has made him.

Õnnepalu's short work is a powerful statement of a condition that many a victim of imposed physical and emotional deprivation must suffer: a self that denies itself all the joys of life, a self so deeply in pain that it can only seek to destroy its own being.

San Francisco, 2000

Starting Over

STACEY LEVINE **FRANCES JOHNSON: A NOVEL**
(ASTORIA, OREGON: CLEAR CUT PRESS, 2005).

Stacey Levine

About a third of the way through reading Stacey Levine's new novel, *Frances Johnson*, I commented to a friend that, unlike so many American fictions which seem to plow through plot and character like a thresher moving down rows of corn (if rows might be understood as chapters), this was a wonderfully lazy narrative, a story that seemed to have no particular place to go and all the time in the world to take you there.

The jacket cover of this Green Integer-size paperback compares Levine's writing to that of Jane Bowles, and there is a certain truth to that observation, particularly in the eccentricity of Bowles's characters who act less out of determination than from whim and behave with an almost passive acceptance of forces beyond their control. Behind Bowles's writing, however, there are generally exotic, strange worlds (Panama, Guatemala, Morocco, etc) that transform or at least *inform* both characters and text. Although Levine has set her new fiction in Florida with a nearby volcano to possibly stir things up, the small town of Munson — despite the daily rumblings of the natural forces around it — is a drab world of dirt and mud. Buildings, streets, homes, and general landscape are rarely described, and when they are it merely confirms the feeling that the town and its citizens are perpetually in a fog, enervated, unable to act. Accordingly, the fiction, unlike more normative realist presentations with emphasis on place, centers itself on character—particularly upon the thinking processes of its central figure, Frances Johnson. And it is the languid revealing of this figure that seems to slow the story down and to allow it to move in the multiple directions in which Frances feels driven and pulled.

Midway through the book, as Frances arrives at the house of her close friend Nancy (a house, incidentally, which the author *does* describe and observes it as being "lovelier than any dwelling in Munson, and perhaps for this reason folks bore her [Nancy] grudges"), Levine admits to the very method of storytelling I had noted:

"Frances, you recently told me you had several dreams about chopped onions," and Frances nodded rhythmically, smiling happily as the two women found the thread of a familiar, meandering dialogue that proceded in the halting yet serene manner of a snail crossing a road over hours, unaware of time; and forgetting the time indeed, not interested in turning back, the friends talked, less in a conversation with a point than in a kind of unstoppable practice that neither woman wished to end.

Faced with such a linguistic construction it would be almost pointless to describe the fiction's "plot." The story — for those who must have one — is about a few days in Frances' life in which she suddenly takes stock of herself and feels drawn to make decisions about her life: should she leave the small and grungy town of Munson and enter the world; should she abandon her sexless relationship with Ray Mars, who the rest of the townspeople, including Ray's brother Kenny, feel is not good enough for Frances; should she attend the annual town dance and be swept away in the arms of the new town doctor Mark Carol? These are the issues, along with others, that suddenly face our hero, and are posed, along with questions with which the author directly confronts the reader in her own series of interrogations such as "To which places would Frances Johnson go?"

In search of answers, Frances goes many places: to visit her friend and doctor Palmer, to speak to the owner of the local diner, Mal, and, as previously mentioned, to visit Nancy. Yet none of these people can answer for her, and each helps only to instill yet more confusion as to what she should do. Mal insists she is sick and will die of some dread disease; Palmer encourages her to leave town in search of vast oil deposits that he needs for a balm he has concocted; and Nancy, who Frances suddenly perceives is more ordinary that she imagined, asks her to help out in cleaning and cooking for the impending visit of her children.

In the end none of these choices seem to matter. Frances's mother, a determined small-town woman who in her dominance of her daughter has obviously helped to generate the young woman's passivity, insists that she attend the dance, where Frances is, so to speak, swept away into the arms of Doctor Carol. But even this event has little significance as the author hilariously pulls the rug out from under character and reader by sending the mother back to the clearing where she has left her daughter lying beside both Mark and Ray, to announce that the community has suddenly determined Mark Carol is a no-good "crumb-bum!" "There are others, though, Frances: you'll see." The story, accordingly, has the potential to start over. And the reader—like Frances and Nancy in their conversations—has taken so much pleasure in the telling of the story that, indeed, he is willing to read the book—and experience these few days of her life—again.

Los Angeles, October 25, 2005

Reprinted from *The New Review of Literature*, Vol. 3, NO. 2 (April 2006)

As one can gather from the above review, Stacey Levine is one of my very favorite authors, a writer uncovered, if not "discovered" by my Sun & Moon Press. When I began the press, I personally answered every author who sent us a manuscript; over time, however, it became quite apparent that the writers who sent us work "over the transom," so to speak, had little idea of what we were publishing. During the twenty some years I edited Sun & Moon, I accepted only two manuscripts written by writers I'd never heard of before—and one of those, a collection of stories by Wendy Walker, had come recommended. By 1991 or 1992, when Stacey sent her unsolicited manuscript to us, I was basically not reading new work. Then senior editor Ann Klefstad would, from time to time, take up the stack of unsolicited works, answering each of them with a form letter. But Ann was also a conscientious soul, and she often read parts of the manuscripts before she returned them.

One day, she handed me a small pile of pages, saying, "I think you ought to take a look at this one." Ann was a brilliant editor, and she knew exactly the kind of work I was looking for, so I dutifully packed away the manuscript, taking it home with me. It was a collection of short stories by then unknown writer Stacey Levine.

These tales, needless to say, were extremely compelling, written in a carefully crafted language that stunned me. I immediately accepted the work, and we published the book to some acclaim in 1993 as My Horse and Other Stories. *The collection won the PEN Center USA award for fiction. A few years later, in 1997, we published Levine's first novel,* Dra—, *which immediately sold out of its first printing.*

I first met Stacey in Los Angeles when she attended the award ceremony, and encountered her and her sister again at a reading I gave with Joe Ross in Seattle, her home town. She visited me another time, bringing with her a gift of a snow dome which housed a singing nun, which sits today on my desk. "I think you have the urge to shake up everything from time to time," she announced. Every time I get that urge, I think of Stacey, her wit and wonderful writing as the snow falls upon the singing nun.

Index

GREEN INTEGER
Pataphysics and Pedantry

Douglas Messerli, *Publisher*

Essays, Manifestos, Statements, Speeches, Maxims,
Epistles, Diaristic Notes, Narrative, Natural Histories,
Poems, Plays, Performances, Ramblings, Revelations
and all such ephemera as may appear necessary
to bring society into a slight tremolo of confusion
and fright at least.

*

Individuals may order Green Integer titles through
PayPal (www.Paypal.com).
Please pay the price listed below plus $2.00 for postage to
Green Integer through the PayPal system.
You can also visit out site at www.greeninteger.com
If you have questions please feel free to e-mail the publisher at
info@greeninteger.com
Bookstores and libraries should order through our distributors:
USA and Canada: Consortium Book Sales and Distribution
1045 Westgate Drive, Suite 90, Saint Paul, Minnesota
55114-1065
United Kingdom and Europe: Turnaround Publisher Services
Unit 3, Olympia Trading Estate, Coburg Road, Wood Green,
London N22 6TZ UK

Our titles [listed by author]

James Joyce *On Ibsen* [1-55713-372-7] $8.95

Richard Kalich *Charlie P* [1-933382-05-8] $12.95

Steve Katz *Antonello's Lion* [1-931243-82-4] $14.95

Ko Un *Ten Thousand Lives* [1-933382-06-6] $14.95

Alexei Kruchenykh *Suicide Circus: Selected Poems*
[1-892295-27-X] $12.95

Tom La Farge *Zuntig* [1-931243-06-9] $13.95

Else Lasker-Schüler *Selected Poems* [1-892295-86-5] $11.95

Michel Leiris *Operratics* [1-892295-03-2] $12.95

Osman Lins *Nine, Novena*
[Sun & Moon Press: 1-55713-229-1] $12.95

Mario Luzi *Earthly and Heavenly Journey of Simone Martini*
[1-9312433-53-0] $14.95

†Thomas Mann **Six Early Stories* [1-892295-74-1] $10.95

†Harry Martinson *Views from a Tuft of Grass*
[1-931243-78-6] $10.95

Julio Matas [with Carlos Felipe and Virgilio Piñera] *Three
Masterpieces of Cuban Drama* [1-892295-66-0] $12.95

±Friederike Mayröcker *with each clouded peak*
[Sun & Moon Press: 1-55713-277-1] $11.95

Deborah Meadows *Representing Absence*
[1-931243-77-8] $9.95

Douglas Messerli *After*
[Sun & Moon Press: 1-55713-353-0] $10.95

Bow Down [ML&NLF: 1-928801-04-8] $12.95

First Words [1-931243-41-7] $10.95

ed. *Listen to the Mockingbird: American Folksongs and
Popular Music Lyrics of the 19ᵗʰ Century* [1-892295-20-2] $13.95

Radio Dialogs II [1-892295-80-6] $13.95

The School for Atheists: A Novella=Comedy in 6 Acts
[1-892295-96-2] 16.95

Arthur Schnitzler *Dream Story* [1-931243-48-4] $11.95

Lieutenant Gustl [1-931243-46-8] $9.95

Eleni Sikelianos *The Monster Lives of Boys and Girls*
[1-931243-67-0] $10.95

Paul Snoek *Hercules Richelieu* and *Nostradamus*
[1-892295-42-3] $10.95

The Song of Songs: Shir Hashirim [1-931243-05-0] $9.95

Gilbert Sorrentino *Gold Fools* [1-892295-67-9] $14.95

New and Selected Poems 1958-1998 [1-892295-82-2] $14.95

Christopher Spranger *The Effort to Fall*
[1-892295-00-8] $8.95

Thorvald Steen *Don Carlos* and *Giovanni*
[1-931243-79-4] $14.95

Gertrude Stein *History, or Messages from History*
[1-55713-354-9] $5.95

Mexico: A Play [1-892295-36-9] $5.95

Tender Buttons [1-931243-42-5] $10.95

Three Lives [1-892295-33-4] $12.95

To Do: A Book of Alphabets and Birthdays
[1-892295-16-4] $9.95

Kelly Stuart *Demonology* [1-892295-58-X] $9.95

Cole Swensen *Noon* [1-931243-58-1] $10.95

Fiona Templeton *Delirium of Interpretations*
[1-892295-55-5] $10.95

Henry David Thoreau *Civil Disobediance*
[1-892295-93-8] $6.95

1001 Great Stories, vol. 1, Douglas Messerli, ed.
[1-931243-94-8] $12.95
1001 Great Stories, vol. 2, Douglas Messerli, ed.
[1-931243-98-0] $12.95

† Author winner of the Nobel Prize for Literature
± Author winner of the America Award for Literature
• Book translation winner of the PEN American Center
Translation Award [PEN-West]
* Book translation winner of the PEN/Book-of-the-Month
Club Translation Prize
+ Book translation winner of the PEN Award for Poetry in
Translation

THE PIP [PROJECT FOR INNOVATIVE POETRY] SERIES OF WORLD
OF POETRY OF THE 20ᵀᴴ CENTURY

Volume 1 Douglas Messerli, ed. *The PIP Anthology of World Poetry of the 20ᵗʰ Century* [1-892295-47-4] $15.95

Volume 2 Douglas Messerli, ed. *The PIP Anthology of World Poetry of the 20ᵗʰ Century* [1-892295-94-6] $15.95

Volume 3 Régis Bonvicino, Michael Palmer and Nelson Ascher, eds.; Revised with a Note by Douglas Messerli *The PIP Anthology of World Poetry of the 20ᵗʰ Century: Nothing the Sun Could Not Explain—20 Contemporary Brazilian Poets* [1-931243-04-2] $15.95

Volume 4 Douglas Messerli, ed. *The PIP Anthology of World Poetry of the 20ᵗʰ Century* [1-892295-87-3] $15.95

Volume 5 Douglas Messerli, ed. *The PIP Anthology of World Poetry of the 20ᵗʰ Century: Intersections—Innovative Poetry in Southern California* [1-931243-73-5] $15.95

Volume 6 Peter Glassgold, ed.; Revised and expanded, with a Note by Douglas Messerli *Living Space: Poems of the Dutch Fiftiers* (1-933382-10-4) $18.95

Volume 7 Douglas Messerli, ed., *At Villa Aurora: Nine Contemporary Poets Writing in German* (1-933382-68-6) $15.95